The Christian Revolutionary

The
Christian
Revolutionary:
John Milton

HUGH M. RICHMOND

University of California Press
Berkeley, Los Angeles, London

University of California Press
Berkeley and Los Angeles, California
University of California Press, Ltd.
London, England
Copyright © 1974, by
The Regents of the University of California
ISBN: 0-520-02443-5
Library of Congress Catalog Card Number: 73-76107
Printed in the United States of America

To Phil and Jane Brady,
for many merry meetings
in Cambridge and elsewhere

Contents

Prelude

"The sun was still low as, hesitant as two unbidden guests, we stopped between the columns of the propylaea before this temple, which lay there with the light behind it like a cool and airy silhouette, against which the rock base, lacerated but worn smooth by millions of footsteps rose slowly like a gleaming pathway made by the sun. . . . The lighting is perhaps best in the morning; but after an exhausting day in stuffy museums and in teeming streets the temptation to rest in the marble coolness up here, to watch the sunset sky turn opal blue behind the columns of the Parthenon and the shadows lengthen over Athens, often induced us to make an extra trip up here. . . . There was time for much meditation in the Parthenon's shadow after the first rapture had subsided, *inter alia* the question of the disrepute of classic art. It can hardly be denied that the Parthenon, Praxiteles, and Venus de Milo are, for an increasing number of people, in process of becoming the quintessence of all that is dead, banal and uninteresting. . . . Everything indicates that the development which caused an earlier generation to turn away from Laocoön and Apollo di Belvedere, once so much admired, to 5th century art, is now abandoning "the classicism

of the golden age." . . . Not since the Middle Ages, in
fact, have the Greeks been in such disfavor as in these
latter days. The causes of this "dehellenizing" of our
cultural consciousness are no doubt many and deep
rooted. . . . From the 19th century we have inherited
the idea that art, in a direct or indirect sense, is a
reflection of life, and our own art largely fulfills this
condition: it reflects personalities, expresses the spirit
of the age, represents class consciousness, analyzes psychological or other truth. . . . Against this background,
the commentary on life given us by Greek art is, to
say the least, sketchy and comes perilously near the
really false academic art which was the official mask
of the middle class during the last century. . . . As long
as people believed in reason and spiritual progress they
acknowledged that Greek art specialized in one thing
which none could excel: the portrayal of the highest
adventures of the intellect. It is this last bastion which
is falling, now that people have begun to doubt the
possibility of a clearsighted and exalted intellectual life,
just as they previously ceased to believe in an ideal
material existence. Experience indicates, in fact, that
even in this respect man is doomed to impurity, dubious
dependence, and innate weakness—something which is
proved by a sufficiently thorough survey of the intellectual lives of great men. . . . Plato had a conviction which
is apt to confuse readers of today because it is so utterly
at variance with our own ideas: he held that you can
have knowledge only of what you possess, that, for
instance, only the virtuous can know what virtue is.
The Parthenon says much the same. . . . The fruit of
a slowly clarifying thought—which has never pretended

to originality but, on the contrary, counts it an honour
to be typical—this temple suggests the organic process
which allows all proportions, step by step, to attain their
perfect harmony through the patient presence of an
unbroken effort. . . . The Greeks preferred to make life
of their art; we on the other hand make art of life."

G. Schildt, *In the Wake of Ulysses*
(New York: Dodd, Mead & Co., 1953), 150-155.

1: Precedents and Methods

Göran Schildt's thoughts as he watched the sun rise and set from the Parthenon afford only the most subjective reactions to the increasing de-Hellenization of Western culture; but that process is currently operating at all intellectual levels. Even the Catholic hierarchy is at last reluctantly following the lead of the Reformation churches in de-emphasizing both the Latin traditions which it preserved for nearly two millennia, and the synthesis with Greek philosophy which made Thomas Aquinas the founder of scholastic philosophy. Only in the academic world, as the etymology of that very adjective "academic" implies, is Greek influence still largely pre-eminent in the way Matthew Arnold advocated in *Culture and Anarchy*. The humanistic tradition remains faithful to the Platonic cult of intellect for its own sake, and to a belief that the perfection of individual capacities depends only on the masterful manipulation of ideas untainted by affective or expedient considerations. However, the ineffective yet radical approaches to ethical, social, and political problems resulting from this solipsistic idealism have recently cost the universities dearly in prestige and resources. In the hope of clarifying the interaction of forces leading to this outcome, I propose in part to demonstrate in the following pages some of the consequences of accepting such "Platonic" ideals, as they are displayed in the archetypal career of one of the first great modern intellectuals: John Milton. However, the ultimate goal of my discussion is not to provide a negative illustration of these consequences of his erroneous earlier choices but to show that Milton's ultimate escape from idealism is a central factor in the triumphant art of his three last great poems, whose character specifically derives from his rejection of much of the pagan Greek cult of intellect. It is this final heroic escape that makes him truly exemplary for moderns.

In Milton's earlier career we may see prefigured most of the hopes and problems, expectations and failures, that have dislocated the twentieth century. These precedents are by no means inspiring insofar as they clearly anticipate our own often ruinous experience; yet for many scholars Milton's youthful idealism remains a consistently positive example, as for Arthur Barker when he asserts: "I believe the true influence of his idealism (and his art) will revive because it is from a faith in the ultimate victory of truth such as he possessed that the human spirit must derive the strength to triumph over its enemies in the twentieth as in the seventeenth centuries."[1] Yet even Barker recognizes in Milton's first struggles for reform a "zealous and overly optimistic confidence,"[2] and he concedes that from the start Milton "accepted certain principles without considering their implications, and expressed them with an

[1] Arthur E. Barker, *Milton and the Puritan Dilemma* (Toronto: University of Toronto Press, 1942), p. xiv.

[2] Barker, p. 6.

assurance which represents rather absence than coherence of thought."[3] Among the principles which Barker identifies as characteristic of this dangerous first phase of Milton's career is "the conviction that the human reason, rightly guided, is the image of God in us yet remaining,"[4] derived from the circumstance that "unlike the Calvinist deity, Milton's God was essentially reasonable."[5] Therefore, insofar as Milton "possessed an assurance of divine guidance . . . even in his early poems . . . the most characteristic product of that inspiration was an ordered patterning."[6]

At first sight such an ordering, whether intellectual or artistic, is unlikely to appear pernicious to anyone, and to label it "Platonic" may well seem more specious than definitive, for historically Plato has had an influence as complex and paradoxical as his own subtle and ironic personality. It is not possible to distinguish a single, simple, and definitive Platonic tradition in the West, because his influence has been so richly permutated, not to say distorted or even misrepresented. Therefore, if I seek to show that Milton's early idealism was a costly error both to his life and his art, this is not to suggest that both aspects of his career gained nothing incidentally in sophistication and appeal from the vast range of more or less Platonic sources; and so I am certainly not concerned to argue for the uniformly negative influence of all that Milton ultimately derived from Plato and his inheritors. Nor do I seek merely to invert the values of scholars like Irene Samuel or Molly

[3] Barker, p. xix
[4] Barker, p. 21.
[5] Barker, p. xvii.
[6] Barker, p. xvii.

Mahood,[7] by achieving for Milton's humanism the definitive discredit with which William Empson has sought
willfully and unsuccessfully to invest his Christianity.[8]
Nevertheless, there are specific elements in European
philosophy, at least partly derived from Plato or his
followers, which have often been criticized as socially
and politically injurious, and which are indeed deeply
opposed to the ultimate origins of Christianity—the very
Christianity to which, so paradoxically, they have often
been assimilated from the time of St. Augustine, and
even of St. John's Gospel. The best academic authorities
have themselves shown respect for the modern scholars
by whom the dangers of these elements of "Platonism"
have been demonstrated and powerfully censured.

Perhaps the most plausible, sustained, and deeply
damaging of modern attacks on such aspects of the
ultimately Platonic tradition are to be found in Karl
Popper's *The Open Society and its Enemies*. In this book
we find possible grounds for reversing Barker's confidence that Milton's final worth for us lies in his supreme
concern with "self-discipline in accordance with the
highest dictates of virtue. That lesson we still need to
learn, and he, in some measure, still can teach."[9] It is
precisely for advocating this naively positive educational
role that Popper finds himself most stringently censuring
Plato and his later allies. In order to understand the
analogues in the ultimately repressive and conservative

[7] Irene Samuel, *Plato and Milton* (Ithaca: Cornell University Press,
1947); M. M. Mahood, *Poetry and Humanism* (New Haven: Yale
University Press, 1950).

[8] William Empson, *Milton's God* (London: Chatto and Windus,
1961).

[9] Barker, p. xiv.

roles of Milton and Cromwell in the last tyrannical
phases of the Commonwealth, it is necessary to recognize
the profoundly restrictive consequences of the cult of
ideological excellence which the youthful Milton shares
with Plato (and many other radical yet basically conservative reformers). Both authors were deeply committed
to the supreme importance of education for the well
being of the individual and the state. Popper ruefully
admits that "it has been said, only too truly, that Plato
was the inventor both of our secondary schools and our
universities."[10] But Popper goes on to assert that Plato
"hoped to arrest political change by the institutional
control of succession in leadership. The control was to
be educational, based upon an authoritarian view of
learning—upon the authority of the learned expert, and
'the man of proven probity.' "[11] In such a system
"Plato's fundamental aim was to arrest political change.
. . . When [the members of the upper class] are too
old to think independently, they shall become dogmatic
students to be imbued with wisdom and authority in
order to become sages themselves, and to hand on their
wisdom, the doctrine of collectivism and authori-
tarianism to future generations."[12] In his ultimate, stun-
ningly outrageous recourse to the *argumentum ad hominem*, Popper claims that "we see that nobody but
Plato himself knew the secret of, and held the key to,
true guardianship. But this can mean only one thing.
The philosopher king is Plato, and the *Republic* is Plato's
own claim for kingly power — to the power which he

[10] K. R. Popper, *The Open Society and Its Enemies* (New York:
Harper and Row, 1963), I, 136.

[11] Popper, I, 137.

[12] Popper, I, 133.

thought his due, uniting, as he did, both the claims of
the philosopher and of the descendant and legitimate
heir of Codrus the martyr, the last of Athens' kings,
who, according to Plato, had sacrificed himself 'in order
to preserve the kingdom for his children.' "[13]

Popper attempts to systematize Plato's views under
the guidance of this assumed goal of a conservative
revolution, and quite early on he establishes that Plato
"certainly believed that it is possible for us by a human,
or rather by a superhuman effort, to break through the
fatal historical trend, and to put an end to the process
of decay. . . . It is therefore understandable that the
great cosmic turning-point may coincide with a turning-
point in the field of human affairs—the moral and
intellectual field—and that it may, therefore, appear to
us to be brought about by a moral and intellectual
human effort."[14] The realization of this potentiality is
illustrated in what Popper calls Platonic utopianism:
"Any rational action must have a certain aim. It is
rational in the same degree as it pursues its aim consciously and consistently, and as it determines its means
according to this end. To choose the end is therefore
the first thing we have to do if we wish to act rationally;
and we must be careful to determine our real or ultimate
ends, from which we must distinguish clearly those
intermediate or partial ends which actually are only
means, or steps on the way to the ultimate end. . . .
We must determine our ultimate political aim, or the
Ideal State, before taking any practical action."[15]

[13] Popper, I, 153.
[14] Popper, I, 20.
[15] Popper, I, 157.

I must obviously seem unfair to Plato in refracting his image through the exposition of his harshest modern censor; but it is crucial for any dissenter to recognize that this modern case against Plato is not simply a result of the personal hostility of a single thinker prejudiced against one aspect of his philosophy. The exact parallel to Popper's criticism of Plato as a social scientist can be found in the very different discipline of theology, with Anders Nygren's *Agape and Eros*. Nygren provides a sophisticated modern recension of the Reformation's arguments against the synthesis of classical philosophy and Gospel Christianity, resulting from the syncretic outlook, which helped medieval Catholicism to become the great repository of Western civilization. In the process the historical identity of Jesus became a less exclusive focus almost of necessity, and the scholasticism of the medieval universities recreated the intellectual milieu of the ancient Academy. Nygren's vision of Plato's role in such church history is identical to that of Popper's suspicion of Hellenistic Idealism in its political aspects. Nygren asserts that "quite early in the history of thought we find the great fundamental questions asked concerning the True, the Beautiful, the Good, and—to crown them all—the Eternal. For our Western civilization the formal statement of these questions was the work of Plato.... And ... we are still occupied ultimately with these same great questions today.... It happens, however, from time to time in the historical process that the meaning of one or other of these questions is completely altered. ... It can equally well be a general, underlying sentiment which involves a certain attitude toward these questions. ... In all ages it has been the conscious or unconscious endeavour of metaphysics to blur this distinction. Men have believed that by philosophical analysis the answer could be deduced from the question. At this point there is an obvious difference between the metaphysical systems and every religious outlook. . . . The metaphysician always tries in one way or another to deduce his answer as 'necessary,' while the religious mind firmly refuses to do so, but insists on its answer as axiomatic and thus maintains a synthetic relation between question and answer."[16]

The nonlogical yet dynamic quality of Nygren's sense of "a synthetic relation between question and answer" is clarified by Popper's outline of an intuitive pragmatic system which is to provide a foil for Plato's utopianism. Both modern thinkers feel that successful alterations in society are not just the result of the imposition of human will on experience, but a synthesis of human aims interacting with the intrinsic nature of the reality which lies outside effective human domination or knowledge. This more modest sense of human insight and power leads Popper to expound a contrasting system to Plato's which he christens "piecemeal engineering." Popper explains that in the practice of such an approach to experience "the piecemeal engineer will adopt the method of searching for, and fighting against, the greatest and most urgent evils of society, rather than searching for, and fighting for, its greatest ultimate good."[17] The utopian approach by contrast to this rejects induc-

[16] Anders Nygren, *Agape and Eros* (New York: Harper and Row, 1969), pp. 42-43.
[17] Popper, I, 158.

tion entirely and "recommends the reconstruction of society as a whole, i.e., very sweeping changes whose practical consequences are hard to calculate owing to our limited experiences. It claims to plan rationally for the whole of society, although we do not possess anything like the factual knowledge which would be necessary to make good such an ambitious claim. We cannot possess such knowledge since we have insufficient practical experience. . . . But piecemeal social experiments can be carried out under realistic conditions, in the midst of society, in spite of being on a 'small scale,' that is to say without revolutionizing the whole of society. . . . The mechanical engineer can do all this because he has sufficient experience at his disposal, i.e., theories developed by trial and error. But this means that he can plan because he has made all kinds of mistakes already; or in other words, because he relies on experience which he has gained by applying piecemeal methods. . . . In all matters, we can only learn by trial and error, by making mistakes and improvements; we can never rely on inspiration, although inspirations may be most valuable as long as they can be checked by experience."[18]

It is, by Nygren's standards, no accident that Popper's account of "piecemeal engineering" somewhat resembles St. Paul's counsel in Thessalonians (I.5,21): "Prove all things; hold fast that which is good." In many of his Letters, Paul advocates great caution about rigid and absolute definitions of excellence, whose application usually tends to be counterproductive (1 Corinthians, 8; 9, 19-22; 10, 23-33). And coupled with this skeptical

[18] Popper, I, 161-163, 167.

procedure is his sense of the inevitability of unsatisfactory experience, of uncertainty, and even of mental confusion, all considerations which defy intellectual ordering (1 Corinthians, 1, 17 - 2, 16). With the same sense of indeterminacy as Popper, Nygren rejects Plato's radicalism as contrary in method to most historically documented processes of religious evolution: "At the supremely important turning-points in the history of religion, when something really new appears on the scene, it is curious to observe how the consciousness that the new is emerging is coupled with a conservative retention of the old. . . . It is merely a symptom of the fact that all the really great revolutions begin from within and the new life only gradually bursts asunder the old forms and creates new ones for itself. . . . Luther does not first appear as the founder of a new Church, but he holds on to the old as long as he possibly can; it is only through force of circumstances that his reforming work leads to the formation of a new, independent Church. But the supreme instance is furnished by the emergence of Christianity itself. . . . Jesus does not come forward as the founder of a new religion; and yet Christianity develops into something altogether new and different in kind from Judaism."[19] This same conservative mode of advance is also very characteristic of many phases of the Reform Movement in England, and is the underlying motive governing its evolution up to the time of Milton.

Such an evolution in any phase of church history is necessarily discontinuous, fragmentary, painful, and even at times ridiculous; as Paul says, "It is written:

[19] Nygren, p. 67.

'I will destroy the wisdom of the wise, and the prudence of the prudent will I reject.' For consider, what have the philosopher, the writer, and the critic of the world to show for all their wisdom? Has not God made the wisdom of this world look foolish? . . . For the Jews ask for miraculous proofs and the Greeks an intellectual panacea, but all we preach is Christ crucified—a stumbling block to the Jews and sheer nonsense to the Gentiles" (I Corinthians, 1, 19; Phillips). Any religion which founds its central convictions on such a subject as the ghastly event of the crucifixion clearly rejects the idea of salvation by reason. Nygren asserts that such episodes prove that by its origins Christianity is essentially opposed to sustained systematic thinking or even any reasoned calculation of merit: agape is "spontaneous and unmotivated. . . . God does not love that which is already in itself worthy, but on the contrary, that which in itself has no worth acquires worth just by becoming the object of God's love. Agape has nothing to do with the kind of love that depends on the recognition of a valuable quality in its object. Agape does not recognize value, but creates it."[20]

I hope that what is beginning to emerge is a sense of two polarized types of personality, not merely two contrasting philosophies or social ethics. On the one hand we have the truly Erotic radical, mystical and revolutionary, whose ultimate excess is so vividly evoked by Denis de Rougemont: "A lover with his beloved becomes 'as if in heaven'; for love is the way that ascends by degrees of ecstasy to the one source of all that exists, remote from bodies and matter, remote from what

[20] Nygren, p. 78.

divides and distinguishes, and beyond the misfortune
of being a self and even in love itself a pair. Eros is
complete Desire, luminous Aspiration . . . to the extreme
exigency of Unity. But absolute unity must be the
negation of the present human being in his suffering
multiplicity. The supreme soaring of desire ends in
non-desire . . . a desire that never relapses, that nothing
can satisfy, that even rejects and flees the temptation
to obtain its fulfilment in the world, because its demand
is to embrace no less than the All."[21] By contrast to
this ambitiously absolutist temperament, Auerbach describes in *Mimesis* the complex discontinuities of reality
reflected in the "multilayeredness" of the individual
characterizations in the Bible. Auerbach asserts that
"the true heart of the Christian doctrine—Incarnation
and Passion—was totally incompatible with the principle
of the separation of styles [into the elevated or sublime,
and the mundane or realistic]. Christ had not come as
a hero and king, but as a human being of the lowest
social station. His first disciples were fishermen and
artisans; he moved in the everyday milieu of the humble
folk of Palestine; he talked with publicans and fallen
women, the poor and the sick and children. Nevertheless,
all that he did and said was of the highest and deepest
dignity. . . . And the most moving account of all was
the Passion. . . . It engenders a new elevated style, which
does not scorn everyday life and which is ready to absorb
the sensorily realistic, even the ugly, the undignified,
the physically base."[22]

---

[21] Denis de Rougement, *Love in the Western World* (Garden City:
Doubleday, 1957), pp. 51-52.

[22] Eric Auerbach, *Mimesis* (New York: Doubleday, 1957), pp. 10,
63.

These divergent strains of thought, so conveniently epitomized by the New Testament and Plato, have been shown by the combined energies of distinguished scholars from broad yet different disciplines, like Popper, Nygren, and Auerbach, to underlie many of the great intellectual systems and literary artifacts associated with the last two millennia of European culture. After recognizing such diverse yet imposing authorities, one may surely consider it probable that the tension which they describe is a key factor in many of the intense debates that have rent the fabric of Western society. For example, despite Augustine's initial debts to Neoplatonism, we can see his shift away from it in such controversies as those between Augustine's ultimately "Pauline" sense of human insufficiency on the one hand, and the relatively far more rationalistic optimism of the various "heretics" whom he combatted: the Gnostics, Pelagius, the Donatists, and others. The pursuit of "Platonic" idealism and its associated emotional ecstasy may also underly that elusive cult which was so murderously extinguished in the genocidal Albigensian Crusade, by means of which Pope Innocent III sought to eradicate the Catharist heresy from medieval Europe. Even the confrontations of the Reformation serve chiefly to contrast Luther's (and Calvin's) sense of human inadequacy with the refined ratiocination of the Catholics' late scholastic philosophy. And the same tension survives into the Age of Reason, and our own Age of Revolution, for it is indeed the occasion for Popper's impassioned analysis of contemporary political ideas and historical theory.

This outline of a highly structured (not to say Structuralist) approach to Occidental political, intellectual, and artistic personality provides me with the underlying concepts of the present book: for Milton was, by training, environment, and temperament, the archetype of the European intellectual and his extreme blend of learning and self-awareness ensures the relevance of both these great Western traditions to any understanding of his mind and art. Milton's highly deliberate career characteristically depended on epic synthesis and consolidation of European intellectual traditions to vindicate its achievement fully. Only if he could show that he had totally assimilated the past could he hope to vindicate all the epic claims and aspirations which he set out for himself from the very start of his career as artist, citizen, and Christian. Implicit in Milton's consistent vision of the poet's obligation to assimilate the past fully, there is a certain view of the nature of all creativity—a view which sees Western culture as necessarily an unbroken continuum. This sense of intrinsic continuity was as true, in Milton's time, of the secular, humanist tradition steeped in the pagan classics as it was of the Christian's sense of his dependence on a direct inheritance of the original revelations recorded in the New Testament. To most Renaissance intellectuals, the lack of either the texts of the pagan classics or of the Bible would have denied him an essential component for the creation of the distinctive European identity.

Implicit in this syncretic view of culture are deep doubts about the creativity, consistency, and rationality of the human mind. The Dark Ages show how easy it is to lose knowledge, and how impossible to reinvent it: only the republication of ancient pagan and Christian texts restored Western culture. Thereafter creative misunderstanding of such established authority often proved a more likely mode of progress than wholly original thought. We have already seen Nygren observe that most revolutionaries are really not progressives but radical conservatives, as with both the "New" Learning and the Christian Reformation. By this interpretation, truly new knowledge usually comes from two humble sources: unintentional misreadings of the past which happen to prove better than the "correct" original, and sheer unprovoked accident (which together cover an astounding amount of modern knowledge, from Columbus mistakenly rediscovering the Americas instead of Asia to Fleming's happy accident with penicillin). Often as with Wycliffe and Luther (not to mention Freud and Marx), the "discoverer" may not really understand what he is bringing about (a painful state of mind well illustrated dramatically in Hamlet's wavering intuition of a new ethic superior to the *lex talonis* justifying the vendetta thrust upon him). It is even less likely that such minds at their moments of discovery will be understood by their contemporaries, who, almost inevitably, will not fall victim to the same random accident or mistake which triggered the involuntary revelation. Holding this pessimistic view of human creativity, one is not surprised that Socrates is poisoned, Christ crucified, and Joan of Arc burned; or that Roger Bacon, Priestly, and other scientists were hounded by their colleagues; or that Dante, Voltaire, Byron, and Hugo were driven into exile. Unconventionality persisted in is viewed by normal minds as an aberration requiring ostracism, and ultimately extermination; only conservative rebels are allowed to flourish (that is why the

modern radical left, often so unoriginal, appeals to
conventional academics and journalists).

Approached in the spirit of such a point of view as
I have just outlined, the career of John Milton becomes
crystalline in its logic and inevitability. One can recognize the devoted orthodoxy of the youthful Milton,
whose very strenuousness in pursuit of traditional virtues makes him prone first to a conservative radicalism
and only thereafter to an involuntary and painful originality which finally cuts Milton off not only from a
superficial innovator like Laud, but even from the conservative rebellion of the Presbyterians. At this point
Milton achieves his characteristic breakthrough to new
awareness: not just a recognition that "New Presbyter
is but Old Priest writ Large," but the sense that *no*
external authority can be trusted to arbitrate one's
judgments, which gives *Areopagitica* its unique value
to later generations. Milton was driven to this involuntary awareness by the censorship of his own pamphlets
advocating divorce (in turn resulting from his unrealistic
expectations of conventional marriage), a pattern which
is true to a more or less Diffusionist expectation, the
view among anthropologists that discovery is unique and
accidental, not a rational, and therefore universally
recurring sequence such as Platonists would predict.
That Milton denied freedom of expression to Catholics,
and later for a full year became Cromwell's press censor
of the *Mercurius Politicus*, does not prove him dishonest,
but merely shows the difficulty of handling an original
idea, even for its expositor.

Such confusions abound in the Renaissance. We can
even link the involuntariness and accidental nature of

more major discoveries of the period to the Reformation Christian's sense of the singularity of the New Testament, which he feels rightly to be alien alike to the pagan culture it supplanted and to the Old Testament tradition it aspired to consummate. But the New Learning of men like Erasmus also approached classical texts in almost the same reverential spirit as it did those of biblical scholarship, even though the pagan texts themselves did not correspond to the religious attitudes of their Christian editors and translators. In particular, the Greek intellectual tradition increasingly reinforced elements incidentally accumulated by Christianity, which were at best indifferent and often (as Nygren shows) alien to the gospel of the New Testament. For if faith in the superiority of God's grace to the inadequacies of human effort is as essential to Christianity as Paul, Augustine, and Luther assert, then the principal value of human reason probably lies in its power merely to discredit itself. By contrast the recension of Plato propounded by Neoplatonists like Plotinus and his followers assumed the self-sufficiency of human reason for the attainment of perfection. By taking enough thought, man could discover the infinite delights of understanding the world, as the *Meno* itself illustrates when the slave boy "spontaneously" discovers that he knows geometry. Such a view assumes the possibility of predictable discovery. By this view, humanity everywhere shares the same potentiality to scale reason's golden stair to the truth. The more secular humanists thus tended to postualte that the New World of the Americas would have spontaneously duplicated the norms of the ancient ages: More, Montaigne, and Rous-

seau all visualize the New World as the plausible setting
for a universal and natural self-cultivation of a rational
kind. The Golden Age was inevitably to be recaptured
in the Age of Discovery.

As de Rougemont illustrated, one of the ironies and
subtleties of Plato's original exposition of his ideas lay
in his skillful assimilation of emotional, indeed sexual,
drives to his educational methods. Not only was there
the motive of ambition to attain divine insight into the
universe, and esoteric pride as an initiate ("Nongeo-
meters keep out"), there was also the aesthetic satisfaction of the cult of beauty and symmetry, and the
sublimated sexuality on which this was so skillfully if
riskily founded in the *Symposium*. (This technique of
repression has produced some paradoxical modern
usages in the divergence between the associations of
"Platonic" love and the skeptical use of "erotic" to mean
the opposite of that spiritual appetite—the ultimate and
all-too-rare refinement of the Platonic Eros). Above all,
as a Pythagorean, Plato exploited the mystical self-in-
toxication of which mathematics was the ritual (rather
than just an instrument serving the sciences as we now
tend to think of it). We can see the continued currency
of this pattern of esoteric mystical scholarship in the
vein of Lovejoy's History of Ideas, which is still pursued
by modern literary academics who track the Jungian
archetypes of reality through the variables of the mundane world, and who most prefer to pursue examples
of that Platonic ladder of perfection which Lovejoy
identifies as "the Great Chain of Being."

If the supposed universality of the Platonic ladder
of perfection illustrates the attitudes of the rationalist

with his high expectations of human capacity to scale the heights of knowledge on its own initiative, the more pessimistic view of creativity finds ready expression in the biblical sense of a needful revelation transcending the willful ineptitude of humanity—compensation for the disabling doctrine of Original Sin. In the pagan world of Plato, aristocracy is the natural mode, readily evolving into the meritocracy which humanist education has successfully imposed on the Western world and which has remained largely unchallenged until the campus disorders of the sixties. But if St. Paul asserts correctly that discovery is beyond prediction and insight is involuntary, then it is no longer possible to justify social or intellectual hierarchy: as Auerbach noted, a band of inland fishermen led by a carpenter's son is just as likely to change the history of the world as a boy trained by Aristotle—indeed it now appears to us more likely that spontaneous movements of the people transcending individual will and capacity may mark the decisive turning points in history. From this point of view, formal education and social sophistication are at best incidental to significant action and insight—the child of a Stratford glovemaker is as probable an author for the world's greatest poetry, if not more so, than a highly educated and socially prominent lawyer like Francis Bacon.

The struggle between these two views of human nature, with their implied relationships to the cosmos, has never been settled, even though the positions have often been confused, and misrepresented, while their specific terms were largely forgotten. In the detailed historical phases of *Agape and Eros* Anders Nygren shows far more authoritatively than I can how from its start the Christian Church struggled to clear itself of the compromise with Greek thought, initiated by Hellenized Jews at least as early as Philo and developed by the Gospel of John, in which the nature of Christ becomes less the expression of a spontaneous love superior to the claims of merit in its application, and more that of the abstract *logos*, an intellectual principle mediating between base reality and the ultimate intellectual truth of the Godhead. This tension with Greek ideas has existed throughout the development of Christian theology; it is the Platonic element in Christian tradition which has spun off most of the great heresies in which Jesus becomes less an incarnation of spontaneous revelation to the humble than the teacher of virtue to the initiate, and, indeed, so much more a paradigm than a person that some of the Gnostics even reduced his historical incarnation to a mere insubstantial vision. We can see the persistence and power of the Platonic strain of intellectual ambition in opposing the flow of spontaneous affection for the humble and inadequate found in agape, when we look at even so "Christian" a work as Dante's *Divine Comedy*. There Jesus is never shown in his humble, historical, or humane gospel nature, and even grace is incarnated chiefly in the complacent theology of Beatrice, who refuses to demean herself by sinking down all the way to Dante's mundane level, or to visit Hell as the Christ did.

Inevitably, the English Renaissance was not exempt from such ambivalences in its thinking and attitudes. The ratiocinative techniques of scholasticism were the medieval analogue to Platonic thought despite their Aristotelian derivation, and during the seventeenth century these were steadfastly preserved in Oxford and Cambridge, even reinforced by Ramism and the contemporary revival in mathematics. This revival may have derived more immediate importance from the practical needs of navigation and engineering, but mathematics were to recover rapidly their mystical Pythagorean value for the religious personality of a Henry More or a Newton. The trust in reason of worthy Anglicans like Richard Hooker diffused in the seventeenth century at least as far as the Cambridge Platonists, a nominally puritan group whose blending of Christian pragmatism with a temperate Platonic ecstasy provided the psychological foundation of the coming Age of Lockian Reason. It was in their subtle, delightful, yet ambivalent intellectual company that their contemporaries Milton and Marvell attained maturity. However mechanical and archaic the University of Cambridge might be in its more formal exercises, the personalities characterizing colleges like Christ's and Emmanuel diffused a sense of enlightened puritanism more significant to the future of their best graduates than any systematic course of studies could ever be.

By breeding, Milton thus stands at the start of his career as heir to the two great contradictory yet complementary traditions of European thought. By education and intellectual association he was a disciple of deliberate reason, in the tradition derived in part from Greek sources like Aristotle and the Platonic Academy, and yet by family influence he was a professed Christian in the selective tradition of intuitive Protestantism. This puritan spirit had aspired to purge religion of just those elements of pagan superciliousness and sophistication which had reappeared in scholastic philosophy, esoteric ritual, and a hierarchical church. The interaction of these two frames of reference defines not only the ideological content of Milton's prose pamphlets, but the nature of his political career and its failure. More important, the final resolution of this great internal debate in his own mind is what lends substantial modern meaning and structure to *Paradise Lost*: for the conclusion that the pursuit of universal, ideal, or divine knowledge is both neurotic in its derivation and pernicious in its consequences is demonstrated in the epic with a painful vividness to which modern intellectuals should be deeply sympathetic. Only in *Paradise Regained* will a new archetype of a purely pragmatic, ethical and political psychology emerge. This model provides the norms of awareness necessary for the successful modern revolutionary, whose potentially cataclysmic powers are unexpectedly illustrated in the Old Testament theme of *Samson Agonistes*. These lessons about effective change were learned by Milton's contemporaries and successors. Headed by Marvell, they helped to bring about the successful Whig revolution which began in 1688 and led thereafter, inevitably if unwittingly, to the creation of modern democracy. By its conditioning of English personality for the next two hundred years, Milton's verse (unlike his prose) was even more crucial than Marvell's in this educative role, and it is only in the present century that we have at last begun to lose the capacity to respond to it accurately and sympathetically. This book is dedicated to restoring some of that responsiveness and the political effectiveness of which it is the essential correlative.

2: Milton's Context and Persona

There were two revolutions against the Stuarts in the seventeenth century; one failed, the other succeeded. It is a wry comment on the invisibility of true success that everyone knows of the one, led by Cromwell and defended by an overconfident Milton, which was a murderous failure; but few except historians pay much attention to the "Glorious Revolution" of 1688, which peacefully put an end to Stuart pretensions, established a modern limited monarchy, and led to the defeat of Louis XIV's megalomaniac plans for Europe. In many ways, the ultimate triumph of the policy of the supplanter of the Stuarts, William III, over that of their French patron reflects the defeat of rational absolutism, in the vein of Plato, by the spirit of pluralistic pragmatism favored by Locke, or later by Popper: a dashing, centralized despotism was defeated by a miscellany of lesser opponents led by William, a man largely lacking in the flair and glory of *le Roi Soleil*. And with the final neutralization of Louis' ambitions in 1713, long after William's death, by the Treaty of Utrecht, there came the attenuation of the influence of all those intellectual aspirations of the French court which had once appeared to be the model for European civilization. The Age of Reason lost the possibility of its full political correlative in a French Empire of Europe, a disaster which was fortunately delayed for another century (and ultimately defeated even then by British pragmatism).

As a cultural rallying point, the personality of William III must seem an anticlimax after the incisive dictatorship of Cromwell and the sly picturesqueness of Charles II, but William's policies are not the less significant, or less definitive, for being undramatic and cautious. His absolute refusal to seize the English crown with the kind of romantic gesture so attractive to the Stuarts and their Cavaliers was founded on the sense that real revolutions succeed in exact proportion to this power to conform outwardly to existing institutions. William did not become king of England, as he might have done, by the absolute right of his military conquest and with unlimited powers, but in full conformity to plodding English tradition and precedent. Effective opposition thus found limited formal grounds on which to challenge him, and could draw on no deep-seated resentment; left only the claims of idle sentiment, the two Stuart attempts at renewed Restoration in 1714 and 1745 had little basis in popular support and were doomed to dramatic failure not unlike Satan's in *Paradise Lost*.

Looking at Milton's own career after 1660, we can see how his responses to the collapse of the Commonwealth prefigure both the achievement of 1688 and the subdued leadership of William III which ensued. It is obvious that Milton has invested Satan with the sweeping dogmatism that he had associated with Charles I in the account of the tyrant in *Eikonoklastes,* but Satan possesses also many of the absolutist traits which Milton came to detest even in Cromwell's erstwhile allies, as they dramatically fell off from loyalty to the Common-wealth to left and right. The alienation we sense from the rebellion of the diabolic chieftain against the will of God derived both from Milton's hatred for an absolu-tist king rebelling against the laws of his own kingdom, and from the author's increasing distaste for the solip-sism and egomania of the more extreme and violent puritan sectaries, whose sweeping ambitions and incom-petence helped to precipitate the Restoration of the Stuarts. Nevertheless, just as there are hosts of modern admirers of Louis XIV's romantic absolutism, like the late Nancy Mitford, and few devotees of the plodding effectiveness of William III, so we have fashionable misreadings of *Paradise Lost* in the vein of Blake and Shelley, which assume that we shall surrender to Satan's fascination with absolute power, while the same senti-mental critics recoil in disbelief or bewilderment from the severe restraint and moderation of Christ in *Para-dise Regained.* Such critics refuse to see that Satan's conspicuous entropy, his waste of energy in useless gestures of authority and empty rationalistic rhetoric, are the manifest signs of an inferior political perform-ance, while Christ's full efficiency leaves little visible evidence of waste in fieriness, smoke, and general pollu-tion. Christ has the near invisibility of the successful revolutionary whose energies are fully invested in signif-icant action, not in empty heroic drama. The self-pitying resentment resulting from Satan's frustrated ambition is too negative and limited a basis for successful reform—

something deeper and more positive is essential.

Hence comes the mature Milton's sense of Christ's doubt that mere mass emotion among the outcast will provide the foundation for revolution (*P. R.* III.47-57, 414-432). More successful revolutions have been derived from the desire of the prosperous to preserve and subtly develop their own power and wealth than have come from the need of the starving and dispossessed to acquire minimum standards. Even Milton's own sustained career as an intellectual and a Commonwealth supporter was financed by the comfortable private income derived from his father's successful career as a scrivener. As Marx rightly perceived, a prosperous society is needed not only to afford the material basis for dynamic revolution, but also before the case for change can be developed ideologically and culturally. The creative intellectual tensions and cultural florescence of the Renaissance and Reformation were in fact mostly fostered by the pressure of mercantile expansion on the established ideas of the time. As the Europeans' physical horizons expanded, so did their historical and artistic ones, and it became fashionable to study alien cultures, whether of the newly discovered Americas or the ancient East, as well as the antiquities of classical Europe. Archeology, antiquarianism, and the dawn of modern systematic history all appear about the time of Milton's birth. And this sense of substantial and attractive alternatives to the contemporary European patterns developed in Renaissance men a new sense of the relativity of values and the possibilities of choice and rejection of current modes of behavior and thought, a trend evident as early as the writing of Machiavelli's *Prince*.

When this new discrimination and historical awareness were applied to religion, they opened up a whole
fresh area of investigation, uncertainty, and divergent
options. The clash between ecclesiastical tradition, contemporary practice, and the newly re-edited Bible in
vernacular tongues was intensified by the evolution of
printing techniques and distribution. For a man like
Luther, it was this new scholarship that opened up a
whole range of discrepancies among the various conventional authorities, discrepancies on which only individual judgment could arbitrate. A very special kind of
self-discipline is required to accept the coexistence of
incompatible systems, and such restraint was denied to
Luther. The supplest English minds of the seventeenth
century were nevertheless capable of it at least occa-
sionally. Not only could an eccentric provincial doctor
like Thomas Browne recognize the need for a tolerant
relativism in religion unacceptable to most of his contemporaries, but a similar sense of the inevitability of
a pluralistic society is the most redeeming feature of
Cromwell's own final political position, a position which
was, ironically, so alien to many of his compatriots that
the only way he could prevent them from cutting each
other's throats was to threaten to do this himself. The
Europeans of the seventeenth century oscillated involuntarily between reluctant acceptance of the loathsome
need to differ peacefully, enshrined in the Treaty of
Westphalia, and abrupt confident relapses into the hope
of enforced unity. Such a hope motivated the revocation
of the Edict of Nantes by Louis XIV in 1685, and
destroyed the assimilation of the Huguenots in France,
stabilized by that edict for nearly a century.

These two phases of seventeenth-century personality must remind us once more of the classic dichotomy, established in my previous chapter, between a relentless insistence on human rationality and the skeptical tolerance of unreliable individual intelligence and capacity required of Pauline Christians. The society of France, under Richelieu's steely discipline, committed itself to many of the ideals of the Platonic state in the form of a homogeneous and centralized society, which inevitably repudiated and repressed both its own "puritan" Catholics—the Jansenists with their mistrust of human reason—and its Protestant sects who repudiated all ecclesiastical authority. The founding of the Académie Francaise in the seventeenth century conforms to the same model, for Plato makes Socrates assert in *The Republic* that if man is rational he should tightly regulate all aspects of his experience, including the very forms of poetry. There is a significant contrast between the martinet spirit of the Académie created by royal fiat to regulate the world of letters, as it did in "la querelle du *Cid*," and the Royal Society which was honored with a patent only after it had established itself spontaneously in England as an informal center of scientific debate. At a very high cost, the English by 1660 had learned to mistrust governmental regulation of thought; for they could no more trust the good sense of those presbyterian reformers who overthrew Charles I than that of his equally doctrinaire henchmen, Strafford and Laud.

However, as late as the publication of *An Apology for Smectymnuus* in 1642, we can see that Milton was still naively addicted to many of the intellectual orthodoxies associated with the political establishments of the day. Above all, he still put considerable trust in the willpower of the human personality, which seemed to him able to structure itself ratiocinatively, along lines implicit in the Socratic dialectic of what Milton calls "the divine volumes of Plato." Milton says that by such readings he "was confirmed in this opinion, that he who would not be frustrate of his hope to write well hereafter in laudable things, ought himself to be a true poem; that is, a composition and pattern of the best and honorablest things; not presuming to sing high praises of heroic men, or famous cities, unless to have in himself the experience and practice of all that which is praise-worthy."[1] The alien sound this sweeping and heroic ethical discipline has to modern ears indicates how completely such a highly systematized view of art has since been undermined, both by the definitive collapse of rational absolutism in the West resulting from the triumph of skepticism, and by the impact of behaviorist psychologies, whether Freudian or Marxist.

Just where Milton's idealism at this time is to be placed on the axis between Platonic Eros and Christian Agape is clarified when he goes on in the same passage to stress that his "riper years and the ceaseless round of study and reading led me to the shady spaces of philosophy; but chiefly to the divine volumes of Plato . . . where . . . I learnt of chastity and love, I mean that which is truly so, whose charming cup is only virtue

[1] John Milton, *Complete Poems and Major Prose*, edited by M. Y. Hughes (New York: Odyssey, 1957), p. 694. For convenience, all later Milton quotations follow this edition, but with specific page references only for prose.

. . . and how the first and chiefest office of love begins
in the soul, producing those happy twins of her divine
generation, knowledge and virtue." After his enthusiastic account of "such abstracted sublimities as these,"
even Milton shows some sense of anticlimax in claiming
merely "not to be negligently trained in the precepts
of the Christian religion"; and he frankly admits that
"though Christianity had been but slightly taught me,
yet a certain reservedness of natural disposition, and
moral discipline, leant out of the noblest philosophy,
was enough to keep me in disdain of far less incontinen-
cies than this of the bordello." One sees how easily
Milton could be attacked as Augustine attacked Pelagius, or as Whichcote was attacked by his tutor, Antony
Tuckney, for reducing religion to "a kinde of a Moral
Divinitie minted; onlie with a little tincture of Christ
added: nay, a Platonique faith unites to God."[2] Milton's
Cambridge as a whole was inclined to Platonism even
in puritan Emmanuel College. Indeed, in Aubrey's comment on Milton's tutor at Christ's College, William
Chappell, there lies one specific indication of where
Milton might have derived his Platonically optimistic
view of human capacity, for Chapell was rumored to
be an Arian (that is, favoring the attainment of salvation
by personal wisdom, thus minimizing the importance
of grace, and therefore also of Christ's revelation).

There need even be nothing in the least puritan in
the cult of chastity of which Milton makes so much
in his youthful works, and in the public persona which
he creates to foil the slanders in the pamphlets directed

[2] Douglas Bush, *English Literature in the Earlier Seventeenth Century* (Oxford: The Clarendon Press, 1948), p. 343.

against him. A ritual faith in chastity often reflects not merely an ascetic contempt for the pleasures of the material world, but also a complacent superciliousness toward the inept like that of the Manichees or even the Donatists, and this complacency easily evolves into a magical pattern for compelling even the will of the gods. Such an esoteric cult of chastity readily sinks into the practical misogyny and sublimated sexuality to which decadent Christianity itself so readily reverted under celibate priesthoods, in marked contrast to the explicit feminism of all the Gospels, and of Luke's in particular. Nothing could be less suited to the simple and sensual audiences first sought in Christ's mission than Milton's ambitious aim of rehearsing "those celestial songs to others inapprehensible, but not to those who were not defiled by women," though he adds hastily: "Which doubtless means fornication; for marriage must not be called a defilement."[3] In that last phrase we suddenly sense Milton's Christian angel swerving in desperately to save him from the disaster of completely ascetic rationalism under the pressure of his Platonic impulses. For even with this faint qualification, Milton still incredibly enough excludes a great many saints (like Augustine and Francis) from full Christian initiation.

Now it is true that in this *Apology* Milton needed to prove to his contemporary readers that his temperament was quite incompatible with the charge of libertinism made by his opponents, and thus the strenuousness of his cult of chastity in the pamphlet is expedient. But the same cult of chastity, derived from "the old Schools of *Greece*" also appears without such cause, and more

[3] Hughes, p. 695.

than incidentally, in *Comus* (11. 418-475), an idealistic
excursion which again is only rescued from total Platonic smugness by the ultimate need of Sabrina's interven-
tion to save its rigid heroine. The Lady's complacent
contempt for her social inferiors, and her total self-confidence in facing the world's temptations, have very little
Christian humility about them. And it is not totally
irrelevant that Milton's own primness earned him the
nickname of "The Lady" as an undergraduate. In other
words, there is an underlying consistency in the temperament of Milton as we can see it expressed up to
the time of his retirement from public service: it shows
an aspiring idealism scarcely held in check by a faint
sense of traditional Christian humility and by the series
of incidental failures that only became overpoweringly
significant with the final collapse of the Commonwealth,
and, with it, all for which Milton had hitherto worked.

The origins of this highly ambitious and self-conscious
temperament are very easy to trace. The principal
autobiographical factors are deftly summed up in E. M.
W. Tillyard's best book, his study, *Milton*: "Milton's
father, the child of comparatively wealthy Catholic
parents, early forsook the paternal religion, was disin-
herited, and forced to earn his own living. It is likely
that he had small taste for the scrivener's profession,
into which a relative had introduced him; but he accepted the necessity, made a competence, and retired when
conditions allowed. Music was his chief delight; and he
would probably have liked to make this, his lifelong
hobby, into his main business in life. Thwarted himself
of full indulgence in the arts, he seems to have attempted
the nearest compensation, and 'destined' his eldest son,

the poet Milton, 'from a child to the pursuits of Art.'
Milton responded with precociousness, and in the
eleventh year of his age had become (so Aubrey tells
us) already a poet. His appetite for knowledge was so
voracious that after he was twelve he hardly ever left
his studies or went to bed before midnight. One of the
maids had to sit up with him. Not considering the
ordinary school teaching at St. Paul's sufficient, the elder
Milton supplemented it with a tutor. He caused his son
(who remembered it with gratitude) to be taught French,
Italian, and Hebrew, as well as the usual Latin and
Greek. In sum, he was as anxious to instil learning into
his son as Lord Chesterfield to inculcate the graces. He
did not omit the question of a profession, and chose
the Church; not, as it would seem, because he was set
on his son being a clergyman, but because in that
profession his learning would find the widest scope. The
effect of this concentrated care and unremitted pressure
on Milton's powerful, sensitive nature was to make him
believe from a very early age, to make him assume indeed
axiomatically, that he was no ordinary person, but
destined to some high achievement in one of the fields
of learning."[4]

If we look closely at the passage from *The Second
Defense of the English People*[5] from which Tillyard
derives much of this data, we find that Tillyard has
rightly stressed the key role of the elder Milton in
formulating explicit and highly deliberate goals for his
son, but that the original passage displays subtler traits

[4] E. M. W. Tillyard, *Milton* (London: Chatto and Windus, 1949),
pp. 7-8.

[5] Hughes, pp. 828-832.

of the relationship. Milton describes his father as "distinguished for his undeviating integrity"—a slightly oppressive attribute which correlates unfortunately with the son's confession that the academic rigors of his childhood were such that "I was subject to frequent headaches." This childhood seems to have been somewhat of the kind which led John Stuart Mill to nervous collapse through the excessive intellectual pressure of his father. But as Milton's youthful personality was more resilient, and thus equal to a fairer challenge, his success in meeting this may indeed have served to strengthen his sense of his own capacity.

The son's brave face to parental assertion appears most obviously in the Latin poem "Ad Patrem" which veils with classical flourishes what seems like open disagreement on the young poet's choice of career. The father's own taste for music is exploited in the defence of the son's literary pursuits: "What pleasure is there in the inane modulation of the voice without words and meaning and rhythmic eloquence? . . . Do not persist, I beg of you, in contempt for the sacred Muses, and do not think them futile and worthless whose gift has taught you to harmonize a thousand sounds to fit numbers, and given you skill. . . . Now, since it is my lot to have been born a poet, why does it seem strange to you that we, who are so closely united by blood, should pursue sister arts and kindred interests. . . . You may pretend to hate the delicate Muses, but I do not believe in your hatred. For you would not bid me go where the broad way lies open, where the field of lucre is easier. . . . But rather, because you wish to enrich the mind, which you have carefully cultivated, you lead me far away from the uproar of the cities into these high retreats of delightful leisure."[6] The implicit defensiveness in these lines will recur throughout Milton's career. One has the continual sense of Milton's measuring himself against almost unattainable external standards—and (when he is candid) conceding failure.

Thus in "On his having arrived at the age of twenty-three," we find him ruefully confronting just such a sense of defeat:

> How soon hath Time, the subtle thief of youth,
> Stol'n on his wing my three and twentieth year!
> My hasting days fly on with full career,
> But my late spring no bud or blossom show'th.

It is not accidental that God appears pedagogically in this sonnet as "my great task-Master." Even in the sonnet on his blindness a much older Milton still seems at first to think of the Divinity as a stern schoolmaster irritated by a pupil's failure to exploit "that one Talent which is death to hide, / Lodg'd with me useless."

At his most perceptive, as in both these sonnets, Milton ultimately recognizes that the contented acceptance of defeat or ineffectiveness is the mind's greatest achievement: "They also serve who only stand and wait." Even at twenty-three he learns to accept "that same lot, however mean or high, / Toward which Time leads me, and the will of Heav'n." However, this poise and acceptance are by no means uniformly characteristic of the younger Milton, who is more prone to assert his own excellence and success without the least qualification, particularly if anyone else impugns his merit.

[6] Hughes, p. 84.

A certain facility is evident in his account in the *Second Defense* of what happened when his father "sent me to the University of Cambridge. Here I passed seven years . . . with the approbation of the good and without a stain upon my character. . . . After this I . . . retired to my father's house, whither I was accompanied by the regrets of most of the fellows of the college, who showed me no common marks of friendship and esteem."[7] Milton gives no hint in this account of the fact that his behavior was provocative enough for the authorities to have sent him away from Cambridge for a period, in punishment; nor that the fellows' uncommon "marks of esteem" did not extend to the granting of a college fellowship, which would have better fitted his subsequent course of independent study than retreat homewards.

Milton's intended public persona is always that of the eminently rational and deliberate mind, supposedly superior alike to the quirks of fortune and the intuitions of genius. His account in the same place of how he came to write the divorce pamphlets affects a plodding sequence of premeditation: "When the bishops could no longer resist the multitude of their assailants, I had leisure to turn my thoughts to other subjects, to the promotion of real and substantial liberty. . . . When, therefore, I perceived that there were three species of liberty which are essential to the happiness of social life—religious, domestic and civil; and as I had already written concerning the first, and the magistrates were strenuously active in obtaining the third, I determined to turn my attention to the second, or the domestic

[7] Hughes, p. 828.

species. As this seemed to involve three material questions, the condition of the conjugal tie, the education of the children, and the free publication of the thoughts, I made them objects of distinct consideration. I explained my sentiments, not only concerning the solemnisation of the marriage, but the dissolution, if circumstances rendered it necessary.... I then discussed the principles of education.... Lastly, I wrote my *Areopagitica*, in order to deliver the press from the restraints with which it was encumbered." A more detached and rational proceeding could hardly be imagined: it sounds like the drafting of episodes for a new *Republic*. Only one comment here, on the divorce pamphlets, betrays a discrepancy between the avowed and the real motives, for Milton claims here that they "were more particularly necessary at that time, when a man and wife were often the most inveterate foes, when the man often stayed to take care of his children at home, while the mother of the family was seen in the camp of the enemy." It is surely not accidental that while Milton at this time stayed on in staunchly Parliamentary London to educate his young nephews, his young bride fled back to her Royalist parents in Oxford, the center of the King's forces.

Moreover, the divorce pamphlets themselves betray more than a dispassionate concern to outline the issues —indeed they remain worth attention precisely because Milton comes to express in them so intensely the need for psychological compatability in marriage of which he has discovered himself to be totally deprived. One scarcely needs to know of the abruptness of Milton's marriage and its immediate intermission to recognize the subjective resonance in the following painfully self-revealing lines about the pitfalls of indissoluble marriage: "But some are ready to object that the disposition ought seriously to be considered before. But let them know again, that for all the wariness can be used, it may yet befall a discreet man to be mistaken in his choice, and we have plenty of examples. The soberest and best governed men are least practised in these affairs; and who knows not that the bashful muteness of a virgin may ofttimes hide all the unliveliness and natural sloth which is really unfit for conversation? Nor is there that freedom of access granted or presumed, as may suffice to a perfect discerning until too late; and where any indisposition is suspected, what more usual than the persuasion of friends, that acquaintance, as it increases, will amend all? And lastly, it is not strange though many, who have spent their youth chastely, are in some things not so quick-sighted, while they haste too eagerly to light the nuptial torch; nor is it, therefore, that for a modest error a man should forfeit so great a happiness, and no charitable means to release him, since they who have lived most loosely, by reason of their hold accustoming, prove most successful in their matches, because their wild affections, unsettling at will, have been as so many divorces to teach them experience. Whenas the sober man honoring the appearance of modesty, and hoping well of every social virtue under that veil, may easily chance to meet, if not with a body impenetrable, yet often with a mind to all other due conversation inaccessible, and to all the more estimable and superior purposes of matrimony useless and almost lifeless; and what a solace, what a fit help such a consort would

be through the whole life of a man, is less pain to
conjecture than to have experience."[8] Thus John Milton
after a few weeks of marriage!

The passage is one of the more self-revealing and
dramatic that Milton wrote, for it consciously admits
limitations in the resources of its author. At this point
at least, Milton is aware of the dangers of naiveté and
of the inexperienced pursuit of simple hopes. Authentic
virtue is not rewarded as Plato predicated. On the other
hand, the costliness of his resolutions never deterred
Milton for an instant from pursuing them, long after
other men would have regarded persistence as futile.
His intransigence at Cambridge was no passing fancy
softened by graduation. *Of Education* savagely re-
proaches Oxford and Cambridge for the low level of
English learning, because of "time lost partly in too oft
idle vacancies given both to schools and universities;
partly in a preposterous exaction, forcing the empty wits
of children to compose themes, verses, and orations
which are the acts of ripest judgment. . . . And for the
usual method of teaching arts, I deem it to be an old
error of universities, not well recovered from the scholastic grossness of barbarous ages."[9] He attacks his
contemporaries as the debased products of the system,
who are either shallow controversialists, or cynics grossly mercenary in their aims and Machiavellian in their
methods; while "others, lastly, of a more delicious and
airy spirit, retire themselves (knowing no better) to the
enjoyments of ease and luxury, living out their days
in feast and jollity which indeed is the wisest and safest

[8] Hughes, p. 708.
[9] Hughes, pp. 631-632.

course of all these, unless they were with more integrity undertaken."[10] This last surprising concession suggests the future development of Milton's mind, as it becomes more attuned to failure, and sympathetic to alienation. But for the moment, the rest of the pamphlet *On Education* is an arrogant piece of Platonizing in which the human mind is optimistically (not to say ludicrously) conceived as capable of assimilating any and all disciplines. Education is thus seen as sufficient to correct Original Sin for "the end then of learning is to repair the ruins of our first parents by regaining to know God aright."[11] Indeed, in the whole scheme of education presented here, it is startling to find this supposedly Christian and puritan author advocating an almost total dependence on pagan sources and authorities for perfecting humanity. Only one incidental phrase alludes to the possibility of using "the evangelists and apostolic scriptures" as a supplement to the primary training in ethics, which he confidently bases mostly on "Plato, Xenophon, Cicero, Plutarch, Laertius and those Locrian remnants."[12]

Milton's aggressive intransigence as a student and pedagogue seems to be closely associated with this desire to create a modern secular educational system scarcely differentiated in principle from Plato's plans for his oligarchic Guardians in *The Republic*. Ironically, in attacking the archaic and inhumane scholasticism of contemporary universities, Milton was also attacking the sole institutionalized source of Christian education,

[10] Hughes, p. 632.
[11] Hughes, p. 631.
[12] Hughes, p. 635.

however vestigial. Rejected by minds like Milton's, the great medieval universities declined into the apathy of eighteenth-century epicureanism (so vividly portrayed in Gibbon's autobiography) and this decline marked the final collapse of academia as a consistent moral force in society. Ironically also, their modern revival in terms close to Milton's ideal transformed the vestiges of the ancient universities into amoral polytechnics, the mass vocational centers epitomized in Clark Kerr's inhumane multiversity.

Even in explicitly religious matters Milton shows a kind of provocative self-confidence that positively invites disaster. His savage attack on Laudian Anglicanism is the emotional climax of *Lycidas* and involves the rejection of his planned ecclesiastical career. His poetic repudiation of his erstwhile Presbyterian allies as "the New Forcers of Conscience" is to be equally fierce and ruinous to his prospects: he asserts harshly that "New Presbyter is but Old Priest writ large." And on his tour of Italy, he was reproached for this inept intransigence by an acquaintance, "John Baptista Manso, marquis of Villa, a nobleman of distinguished rank and authority, to whom Torquato Tasso, the illustrious poet, inscribed his book on friendship." Manso, on Milton's departure, "gravely apologised for not having shown me more civility, which he said he had been restrained from doing, because I had spoken with so little reserve on matters of religion."[13] Milton has no skill in the Pauline art of "being all things to all sorts of men", for he then goes on to illustrate his bravado in matters of belief: "While I was on my way back to Rome, some merchants

[13] Hughes, p. 829.

informed me that the English Jesuits had formed a plot against me if I returned to Rome, because I had spoken too freely on religion; for it was a rule which I laid down to myself in those places, never to be the first to begin any conversation on religion; but if any questions were put to me concerning my faith, to declare it without any reserve or fear. I, nevertheless, returned to Rome. I took no steps to conceal either my person or my character; and for about the space of two months I again openly defended, as I had done before, the reformed religion in the very metropolis of popery." A sardonic critic might note that, while Milton was thus freely allowed to advocate the overthrow of the papacy in its heartland, yet in vindicating free speech with *Areopagitica*, Milton sought to deny English Catholics similar freedom, observing brusquely of his ideal: "I mean not tolerated popery and open superstition."[14] The same sense of the need for limitation of freedom to the exposition of his own or kindred "heresies" no doubt allowed a still rationalist Milton to become a censor of the press under Cromwell.

One must give Milton his due: however involuntary the basic motive, the divorce pamphlets were also the product of outstanding daring in the climate of the times, involving Milton in direct confrontation with the dominant Presbyterians and by consequence (in *Areopagitica*) in a challenge even to Parliament's supreme authority. The admiration that this courage arouses must, however, be tempered by recognition of the fact that neither campaign had even the faintest chance of success. Nor did the impressive attempt to prevent the

[14] Hughes, p. 747.

restoration of Charles II, when it was already almost inevitable, by the publication of *The Ready and Easy Way to Establish a Free Commonwealth* in 1660. All these activities raise a question which I hope ultimately to answer here: how far should we admire qualities that are so obviously doomed to ineffectiveness? Perhaps what we should admire in *Areopagitica* and the other works is something more intimate and less sententious than their ostensible concerns and methods, which are not made valid by our ultimate acceptance of Milton's aims. What counts in the divorce tracts is then not the immediate and doomed public cause, but the intense private experience that transforms our intimate awareness of the nature of marriage. The true reformer would be most important for what he is, not for what he tried, and usually failed, to do. Milton is more important as an involuntary example than as a deliberate propagandist.

Sometimes of course Milton seems just obtuse, as when he is suddenly released from imprisonment after the Restoration and refuses to pay the fees of the Sergeant-at-Arms; this after barely escaping execution as a Cromwellian regicide! The Sergeant ominously observed that he would just as soon hang the recalcitrant poet as struggle for the money. On the other hand, Milton's ambitious self-discipline to a great cause is a necessary preliminary to his ultimate literary and intellectual achievement, even if the achievement itself also has as its first prerequisite the apparent failure of all his ambitions. Only because Milton proposes the encyclopedic challenge of the epic mode to himself from the start of his Cambridge studies does he have the time

to pick up the tremendous intellectual acceleration
needed to carry through his early intuitions of a literary
project:

Such where the deep transported mind may soar
Above the wheeling poles, and at Heaven's door
Look in, and see each blissful deity . . .
Then passing through the Spheres of watchful fire,
And misty Regions of wide air next under, . . .
May tell at length how green-ey'd *Neptune* raves...

Then sing of secret things that came to pass
When Beldam Nature in her cradle was;
And last of Kings and Queens and *Heroes* old.

Already in these lines "At a Vacation Exercise in the
College" Milton correctly visualizes the climax of his
career forty years later. Such ambitious prescience is
perhaps irritating in its self-assurance yet impressive in
the event—unlike Keats' planning to climax his career
"with a few great plays," which proved a far less legitimate and meaningful goal in the end.

Nowhere do we find better illustrations of the charms
and limitations of Milton's state of mind in the immature and preparatory stages of his career than in the
famous passage in the introduction to the second book
of *The Reason of Church Government.* Here Milton
attempts to create for himself a persona illustrating the
inner virtues of true religion, in contrast to the specious
formality of his Laudian opponents (whose legalistic
position he has attacked in the first book). He is thus
explicitly committed to showing himself as something
more than the virtuously ambitious intellectual who
would impress fellow humanists. It is fascinating to
watch the tension in Milton here between the Christian

humility involved in recognizing the need for God's grace in all worthy achievement, and his consciousness of "academic" virtue in the ambitious Platonic sense: "although a poet, soaring in the high region of his fancies with his garland and singing robes about him, might, without apology, speak more of himself than I mean to do; yet for me sitting here below in the cool element of prose, a mortal thing among many leaders of no empyreal conceit, to venture and divulge unusual things of myself, I shall petition to the gentler sort, it may not be envy to me. I must say, therefore, that . . . it was found that whether aught was imposed me by them that had the overlooking, or betaken to of mine own choice in English or other tongue, prosing or versing, but chiefly this latter, the style, by certain vital signs it had, was likely to live. But much latelier in the private academies of Italy, whither I was favoured to resort, perceiving that some trifles which I had in memory, composed at under twenty . . . met with acceptance above what was looked for, and other things which I had shifted in scarcity of books and conveniences to patch up amongst them, were received with written encomiums. . . . I began thus far to assent . . . that by labor and intent study . . . joined with the strong propensity of nature, I might perhaps leave something so written to aftertimes, as they should not willingly let it die. . . . These abilities, wheresoever they be found, are the inspired gift of God rarely bestowed . . . and are of power, beside the office of the pulpit, to inbreed and cherish in a great people the seeds of virtue and public civility. . . . Those intentions which have lived within me ever since I could conceive myself anything worth to my country . . . urgent reason hath plucked

from me . . . and the accomplishment of them lies not
but in a power above man's to promise; but that none
hath by more studious ways endeavoured, and with more
unwearied spirit that none shall, that I dare almost aver
of myself."[15]

Milton hangs, like Mahomet's coffin, midway between
heaven and earth—aware that unaided by God he can
never reach his goal, yet also smugly claiming that no
one has ever done more to justify success on merit alone.
It is not surprising to find Milton in this ambitious
introduction advocating ideas from the *Republic* such
as systematic military exercises, government regulation
of the arts, and the founding of academies like the French
one to refine English society. God gets the ultimate
credit for civilization, but for all practical purposes
mankind had better act as if success were the certain
reward of industrious merit, and be pretty smart about
following Milton's example. It sounds less as if Milton
acquires power to attain his own future achievement
because God grants it than as if the author has done
his share of the job and now it is up to God not to
deny the appropriate stamp of approval in terms of
realized goals. The note of self-concern modulates here
with surprising ease to the stoic self-righteousness of
the pagan ethic, which is theoretically at the opposite
end of the scale to puritanism. There is surely more
than a little hubris in apologizing to one's reader for
writing something as inferior as the work which that
reader has just chosen to peruse, while promising really
great things for the future, if only Providence will avoid
interfering. Such complacency argues ill for literary

[15] Hughes, pp. 667-670.

creativity, nor is it often associated with political success, and all this hortatory prose is now even less read than its purely subjective interest deserves.

Looking at Milton's life with these views in mind, we see that it corroborates them by its mixture of hasty, idealistic action followed by shocked disillusion and endless failures: the failure to establish himself at Cambridge, the collapse of his marriage, the substitution of pamphleteering for poetry, the alienation from the Presbyterians and Parliament, the loss of sight from overwork, the death of Cromwell, and the end of the Commonwealth. If Milton *had* been executed in 1661, we might have been justified in seeing in his career a cautionary tale of ambitious talent defeated by its own excesses. But hindsight will allow us to see that just as Milton redeemed his whole career in the end not so much in spite of failure as because of it, so throughout all the phases of his life he shows extraordinary powers of recovery, and the literary equivalent of these muted triumphs is surely the most exemplary and valuable resource a great author can transmit to his readers. What is important about Milton is *not* that he is gifted and ambitious, nor that he invariably fails in his major assaults on heaven, but that after the failures he comes creatively to terms with them, showing a new maturity, poise, and understanding—unlike Satan.

3: Orthodox Verse

In his historical context, the youthful Milton appears at first to be less a genuine revolutionary than a coherently conservative moderate. For all his particular challenges to orthodoxy, his shocked indignation on each occasion does not reflect a studied alienation from society so much as amazement that it is not perfectly adapted to him. He never speaks as an isolated genius, always as a representative of orthodox standards. One is less aware of Milton moving away from the establishment than of Laud and Strafford moving English institutions away from *him*. If this hypothesis is true, Milton's youthful verse should mostly lend itself to explication through the more conventional ideologies, ethics, and aesthetics of the time. Indeed, it should illustrate many of the orthodox intellectual attributes he later attacks most strenuously, as has been noticed with bafflement by many scholarly critics.

The differences between Milton and the representative poets of various earlier generations, like Spenser, Marlowe, Donne, and Jonson, thus largely reflect the general pattern of evolution through various shades of neoclassicism to baroque aesthetics. Such a progression may be defined as the continued assimilation of classical models from the initial point of incidental and distorted use, through duplication with antiquarian exactitude, to their confident and systematic redeployment for new aims. Above all, there is an advance both in mastery and independence in the face of the classics. Spenser at best shows little sympathy with the classical spirit, while Jonson treats his sources with cautious reverence; Milton does not hesitate to repudiate even his favorite pagans when they conflict with his needs. Thus in *Areopagitica*: "Plato, a man of high authority indeed, but least of all for his commonwealth in the book of his *Laws*, which no city ever yet received, fed his fancy with making many edicts to his airy burgomasters, which they who otherwise admire him, wish had been rather buried and excused in the genial cups of an Academic night-sitting. . . . Why was he not else a law-giver to himself, but a transgressor, and to be expelled by his own magistrates; both for the wanton epigrams and dialogues which he made?"[1] One may contrast this bold censure with Jonson's reverent concern that the ancients might be reviewed cautiously only so far as the vices of "judging or pronouncing against them be away."[2]

The confidence of Milton and his age in the face of inherited tradition produces a new assertiveness and solidity of structure in all the arts. Baroque works have none of the casual and irregular charms of *The Faerie Queene* or the almost constipated movement of a Jonsonian transposition, not to mention the warped and uneasy tensions of Donne's verse. The rigorous application of the pseudo-Aristotelian cult of the Unities is

[1] Hughes, p. 731.
[2] Ben Jonson, *Timber* (London: J. M. Dent, 1951), p. 8.

typical of the bold structuralism of the Baroque Age. Nevertheless these unities were made to support arabesques of the most extravagant nonclassical kind, whether the sentimental death wishes of *Le Cid*, or the whimsical mood the *The Tempest*, or the alchemical foolery of *The Alchemist*. Milton shows the same blend of rigorous mastery and calculated range of moods very early on in his career, and recognition of this blend of discipline and diversity may change our response to many of his earlier poems, which are less simply Spenserian than is sometimes imagined. There is far less of Elizabethan quaintness or Jacobean grotesquerie in this verse than there is of Augustan planning.

A Lyric Triad

Even a little group of short poems like "At a Solemn Music," "On Time," and "Upon the Circumcision" has calculated complexities. These are not the handiwork of "the last Elizabethan" but "the first modern."

At first sight Milton's suave lyric triad seems as if it were unified only in the spirit of minor exercises in conventional modes, but the sense of them as a deliberate triad is confirmed by the significant interaction and even progression of the thoughts which they invoke. Just as *Il Penseroso* depends on *L'Allegro* through development of shared or contrasting poetic and psychological resonances, so the minor discords of "The Circumcision" contrast with our interest in the harmonious vision of the music poem. This latter occasional lyric comes closest to Spenser's *canzone*, with its "linked sweetness long drawn out." Music is treated here in its medieval philosophic role as an echo of the ultimate cosmic harmony, the music of the spheres: "that undisturbed Song of pure concent." Any earthly concert is seen as a necessary phase of Platonic ritual, enabling mankind to aspire to heaven's harmonies: "That we on Earth, with undiscording voice, / May rightly answer that melodious noise." The intrusion of "disproportioned sin" scarcely disrupts this upward surge, and the poem's sense of the ease of "keeping in tune with Heav'n" is corroborated by the readiness of God's response in restoring men "to his celestial consort." The poem differs from its medieval and Spenserian precedents chiefly in its syntactical poise and rhetorical mastery: the first smooth-flowing sentence covers twenty-four lines with effortless ease and clarity. Musicality becomes wholly compatible with lucid, sequential thought: this is truly metaphysical verse, unlike Donne's tortured mannerism which is usually more dramatic and psychological than coherently expository.

If "At a Solemn Music" illustrates the serene absolutism with which Renaissance Neoplatonism reinforced typically medieval modes, then "Of Time" marks a recognition of the Reformation recovery of a subjective sense of being within the Fallen World. We have moved from Spenser to Donne, whose sonnet "Death be not proud" provides the rhetorical pattern for Milton's repudiation of Time's challenge. There is a shock effect worthy of Donne in the brutal advice to Time to "glut thyself with what thy womb devours," and vivid precision in the image "And Joy shall overtake us as a flood." Nevertheless, Donne's anguished uncertainties are missing; there is a complacent conviction that "our heav'nly-guided soul shall climb" and "all this Earthy grossness quit." This refinement remains largely the Platonic escape into pure intellectuality against which the Nicene Creed resolutely set its face in stressing "the resurrection of the body."

Thus far we have had an almost unqualified vision of heaven, and a sense of the victory over mundane reality which precedes this vision; in the third poem we are reminded as Christians of the painful particularities by which this transcendence actually is accomplished, and these turn out to be far less aesthetic than was recognized in the poem about music. The angels who "so sweetly sung your Joy" must "now mourn." The process of redemption so suavely assumed in the first two poems turns out to involve humiliation and mutilation. The grotesqueness of the subject is surely intentional: the melodious aesthetics of the archaic view of music do not lend themselves to discussion of cutting off an infant's foreskin. The poem brusquely reverses the Platonic ascension, recognizing that the truly creative act involves acceptance of pain and humiliation:

O more exceeding love or law more just?
Just law indeed, but more exceeding love!
For we by rightful doom remediless,
Were lost in death, till he that dwelt above
High-thron'd in secret bliss, for us frail dust
Emptied his glory, ev'n to nakedness;
And that great Cov'nant which we still transgress
Entirely satisfi'd.

The repudiation of humanist terms of reference coincides with a total rejection of Platonic metaphysics. The idea of circumcising Plato's first principle is too absurd for a serious intellectual to consider, and Milton is clearly aligning himself now with St. Paul's message of a redemption which was "folly to the Greeks." Since these three poems were composed about the same time and written out in the above sequence in Milton's own manuscript now preserved at Trinity College, it appears plausible to suggest that the progression which I have just traced in their ideas is significant, even if the order is not preserved in the 1645 edition of Milton's poems. Certainly to print either or both of the first two poems without the third is a minor version of the mistake anthologizers used to make in excerpting the first two books of *Paradise Lost*, giving us the Devil and nothing else. It may perhaps seem fanciful to suggest that Milton has here momentarily almost reached the sensitivity to children of that strenuously anti-Platonic painter Velasquez in such famous realistic portraits as that of the little Spanish princess and her attendants; but the last poem of the triad is certainly the most humane, sympathetic, and Christian in considering the minor misfortunes of the infant Jesus. Moreover, Milton manages to conclude it with a steady look at the harsh fact that greatness of mind means mostly acceptance of greatness in suffering: "but Oh! ere long, / Huge pangs and strong / Will pierce more near His heart."

"On the Morning of Christ's Nativity" *and "The Passion"*

The three early lyrics remain fairly orthodox and impersonal. Their ideas can coexist with an intellectual complacency which has yet to test out Milton's views "on his own pulse." But we may be reassured even after noting the academic rationalism of the pamphlets that

Milton does have the fully articulated apparatus of
Christian thought accessible to him when his artistic
sensibility calls for it. However, Christian attitudes are
not entirely assimilated yet to his emotional needs, for
he finally fails in his attempt, at about this time, to
achieve another more ambitious sequence like the one
just discussed, by bracketing together his odes on
"The Nativity" and on "The Passion." Once again we
have the charming and confident topic of a child's birth
followed by the sombre admonition of an account of
that child's agonized death as an adult; and now the
deliberateness of the progression is stressed by the
author at the start of "The Passion":

> Erewhile of Music and Ethereal mirth,
> Wherewith the stage of Air and Earth did ring,
> And joyous news of heav'nly Infant's birth,
> My muse with Angels did divide to sing;
> But headlong joy is ever on the wing,
> > In Wintry solstice like the short'n'd light
> Soon swallow'd up in dark and long outliving night.

Keats perhaps picked up the fifth line for imitation in
his famous image of "Joy, whose hand is ever at his
lips / Bidding adieu," but the rest of Milton's poem
admits a deep reluctance to confront the theme of
absolute defeat:

> These latter scenes confine my roving verse;
> To this horizon is my *Phoebus* bound. . . .
> > Me softer airs befit, and softer strings.

After a few more struggles with a theme too ominous
and destructive for his present rather shallow optimism,
Milton admits that his mind cannot cope with the

horrifying challenge of the crucifixion: "This Subject
the Author finding to be above the years he had, when
he wrote it, and nothing satisfied with what was begun,
left it unfinisht." This early incapacity to cope with
tragic suffering is typical of the other failures induced
by over-optimism in Milton's social and political experience. It is also characteristic of the ambitious spirit of
the age which increasingly avoids the tragic view of life,
as Paul Hazard has noted in *The Crisis of the European
Conscience*: "people want to turn their eyes away from
the suffering Christ."[3] Only a personality like Rembrandt's, or that of the mature Milton, will have the
courage to face the ultimate failure of the private self
and of conventional reason before the arbitrariness and
hostility of the "fallen" universe.

However, the failure of "The Passion" does not affect
the general approval felt by readers of "On the Nativity,"
even though the poem is left curiously unbalanced by
the preponderance of the Devils' roles in its second half
(which might have been offset if the poem were immediately followed successfully by "The Passion" with its
intended emphasis on the heroic human personality of
the adult Christ). It is very easy to show that the virtues
which have encouraged approval of "the Nativity" reflect its anti-Platonic point of view: the theme is not
an ambitious ascent to the ineffable but the loving
descent of the Divine to the level of mundane reality:

> That glorious Form, that Light unsufferable,
> And that far-beaming blaze of Majesty,
> Wherewith he wont at Heav'n's high Council-Table,

[3] P. Hazard, *La Crise de la conscience européenne, 1680-1715* (Paris:
Fayard, 1961), p. 281.

To sit the midst of Trinal Unity,
He laid aside, and here with us to be,
    Forsook the Courts of everlasting Day,
And chose with us a darksome House of mortal Clay.

The theme of a savior "All meanly wrapt in the rude manger" encourages in Milton a quaint particularity more characteristic of the humble craftsman than the sophisticated academic. Readers have been charmed by touches like the shepherds who "Sat simply chatting in a rustic row," talking of "their loves, or else their sheep." Even more pleasantly undignified is the opening spectacle of the young poet sprinting past the three kings to beat them to the manger with his gift. The humorous modesty of the conclusion also helps to frame the weightier implications of the poem with tenderness:

But see! the Virgin blest
Hath laid her Babe to rest.
    Time is our tedious Song should here have ending.

The poem wisely denies itself all pretension. Thus even the dramatic theme of pagan culture appears mostly in an elegiac mood:

From haunted spring, and dale
Edg'd with poplar pale,
    The parting Genius is with sighing sent;
With flow'r-inwov'n tresses torn
The Nymphs in twilight shade of tangled thickets
    mourn.

In the collapse of classical pantheism we see prefigured the rejection of Greek and Latin culture which is to climax Milton's presentation of Christ in *Paradise Regained*. But even the Christian themes of triumph are modestly diminished in the poem. "The Old Dragon" is not yet fully defeated: the poet has hopes that "Time will run back and fetch the Age of Gold" so that "Truth and Justice then / Will down return to men / . . . And Mercy set between."

> But wisest Fate says no,
>> The Babe lies yet in smiling Infancy
> That on the bitter cross
> Must redeem our loss.

My essential point is that the virtues admired in "On the Nativity" derive from this modest recognition of the Christian rhythm: its acceptance of the humble, quaint, discontinuous nature of experience, which gave the art of anonymous medieval craftsmen a vivid particularity denied to the arid theorizing of the pretentious Schoolmen. Few but scholars and specialists now regularly read even an Aquinas, while millions still delight in the statuary and paintings of the forgotten artisans who were his contemporaries. The Nativity Ode scores with modern readers for somewhat similar reasons: the tender love of the mundane and unpretentious gives it a magnetism denied even the most ambitious theorizing. The goal of all such successful art is surely: "to see eternity in a grain of sand" (or perhaps, in our clumsier modern idiom, to find the most immediate objective correlative).

L'Allegro and IL Penseroso

If the humble is so appealing, then our analysis of *L'Allegro* and *Il Penseroso* might also be transformed by a sense of the implicit values and their effect on the content and manner of the two poems. For even more than the Nativity Ode, they have earned the stamp of popular approval denied to and even rejected by any self-conscious Platonist. It seems generally agreed that the lighter, more naive poem must necessarily precede the more maturely meditative one. Certainly the latter definitively refutes the arguments of its predecessor as invalid, while the reverse is not true because *L'Allegro* is mostly insouciant. What has been less recognized is the implication of this: that the poems are not just neatly parallel illustrations of contrasting temperaments but two phases of an evolving argument about the role of the creative mind. The choice is not between two moods, but two functions of which the moods are mostly corollaries. Very approximately, these functions could be described as the work of the imagination and that of the understanding—illustrating a ratio akin to what I choose to consider the difference between Coleridge's secondary imagination, which provides at best the illustration of truth, and the primary one concerned with direct apprehension of that truth itself.

L'Allegro is a poem about artistic diversion, in both the good and the bad senses: the role of art is seen as essentially recreational—either as proper relaxation during or after effort, or even simple escapism, as with the concluding figure of the widowed Orpheus delighted by music. The relaxed mood of the speaker is established early on in the poem when he wakes in his bed to hear the song of the lark. His morning walk allows him to overhear rural diversions:

> While the Plowman near at hand,
> Whistles o'er the Furrow'd Land,

And the Milkmaid singeth blithe,
And the Mower whets his scythe,
And every Shepherd tells his tale
Under the Hawthorn in the dale.

By late afternoon a stroll affords alternative pleasures like the sound of "the merry Bells" of "upland Hamlets," and adolescents dancing to the music of flutes. Evening is set aside among the beer drinkers for fairy tales of Queen Mab and goblins. The country fold's early move to bed leaves the young intellectual (not unlike Milton) by himself, to recall the delights of London "with mask and antique Pageantry." The climax of these recollections of urban entertainments comes with the thought of a visit to "the well-trod stage" to enjoy a comedy of Jonson or Shakespeare. The poem ends with the theme of lulling music as a sedative "against eating Cares" like those of the lonely Orpheus.

The stress throughout lies on the fancifulness of the distractions which art proposes, a mood shared by the mind of the speaker when he sees "Towers and Battlements . . . Where perhaps some beauty lies." Even the recollections of London verge on fantasy:

Such sights as youthful Poets dream
On Summer eves by haunted stream.

This fancifulness is coupled with an innocent sensuality, beginning with the impregnation of Aurora by Zephyrus. "Mirth's crew," in which the speaker solicits membership, is an uncensured prototype of the mob following Comus. Even the country folk seem chiefly concerned with self-indulgence, eating and drinking, dancing or drowsing. The only figure who is shown hard at work is that wretched goblin who, as a result of the general jollity has to do all the work "That ten-day-labourers could not end." It is typical that the poem ends with the thought that even the artistic craftsmanship of Orpheus did not achieve any real resolution of his problems: the ineffective mood of *L'Allegro* leaves Orpheus forever deprived of his only "half-regain'd *Eurydice*."

While *Il Penseroso* aims at no sweeping rejection of art, the poem illustrates its own point when it insists that art be serious, thought-provoking, and intellectually functional. The speaker now requires the challenge of tragedy, or "sage and solemn tunes ... Where more is meant than meets the ear." Orpheus appears again, not however as the artist failing to clinch his achievement, but as the master able to deploy art valuably, so that he "made Hell grant what Love did seek." Even the rural trance into which the speaker again falls has a different note, struck by the activity of the industrious bee, "That at her flow'ry work doth sing." And unlike *L'Allegro* the poem does not end with this trance, but uses it as a prelude to "the studious Cloister" and the study of astronomy and botany. The culmination lies in the maturing of "old experience," not in sweeping youthful fantasy.

This Baconian conclusion is not fortuitous. *Il Penseroso* does more than insist on the serious worth of art, it stresses the superiority of the products of substantial and practical understanding to works merely dependent on imagination. It is riddled with paradoxes depending on the rejection of conventional aesthetics, and with them that cult of formal beauty which Platonism had used as its first incentive to knowledge. Milton's speaker rejects the ambitious climb up the Platonic ladder to heaven, and stresses the downward movement of a more truly Christian concern for the humble and mundane. This sense that the intellectual's ultimate concern should be with the least spectacular effects is beautifully prefigured in the idea that the greatest brightness affects the eye by appearing to darken it because it is:

> too bright
> To hit the Sense of human sight;
> And therefore to our weaker view
> O'erlaid with black, staid Wisdom's hue.

The figure of Vesta is introduced early, as one who prefers the courtship of the somber Saturn to that of the flashing Phoebus Apollo: the ancient Pantheon of potent deities is thus preferred to the glittering follies of the "feared" Jovian divinities handled so skeptically by Homer and Euripides. Even if the speaker solicits the nightingale's song on his nocturnal promenade, he fails to hear it; and "the wandering moon" proves less a symbol of ecstasy than a warning against mystical extravagance. She appears

> Like one that had been led astray
> Through the Heav'n's wide pathless way.

The solitary stroller is also warned by "the far-off curfew" that he should not be straying abroad but return to his study, where again truth lurks in seeming darkness for "glowing Embers through the room / Teach light to counterfeit a gloom."

The nature of the speaker's studies is clarified by a sense of the dichotomy between Erotic intelligence and that of Agape. Note the bizarre reversal of the Platonic ascent in this archetypal progression of thought?

> keep thy wonted state,
> With ev'n step, and musing gait,
> And looks commercing with the skies,
> Thy rapt soul sitting in thine eyes:
> There held in holy passion still,
> Forget thyself to Marble, till
> With a sad Leaden downward cast
> Thou fix them on the earth as fast.

The wording here seems unusually paradoxical: "commercing" is surely a lowly expression for spiritual communion, and it suggests a mutual bargaining in which the higher power will accommodate itself to the needs of the lower. It is also curious that the intellectual's final thoughts, the ones of most gravity, are seen as "leaden"—that is, pulling strongly downwards toward the earth. The moment of truth completing this revelatory trance again lies in the recognition of the humble and earthly. The parallel with the superiority of the leaden casket in *The Merchant of Venice* is obvious.

The serious mind thus follows true love in finding itself driven to lower its sights from heaven to earth rather than the reverse; and this is true not only of the archetype but also of the poem's speaker too:

> let my Lamp, at midnight hour,
> Be seen in some high lonely Tow'r,
> Where I may oft outwatch the *Bear*,
> With thrice great *Hermes*, or unsphere

> The spirit of *Plato* to unfold
> What Worlds, or what vast Regions hold
> The immortal mind that hath forsook
> Her mansion in this fleshly nook:
> And of those *Daemons* that are found
> In fire, air, flood or underground.

While the intellectual may start at the top of a tower, his will does not exact an ascent thence to a Platonic heaven. Instead he expects Plato's own descent (a movement uncharacteristic of Platonic thought, which always tends to ambitious self-advancement). Plato's role is to reveal celestial truths, but also those sublunary principles whose climax unexpectedly comes in "underground." He is to perform an almost Christian act of condescension to the inferior mortal intellect. Even if the Christian emotion of spontaneous attraction to the humble is entirely missing and the content of the passage remains coldly intellectual, its rhythm of movement remains novel in academic thinking (unless it is seen as verging on the degenerate magic of a Dr. Faustus with its parody of religious invocation).

After the ecstatic musical trance with which the poem approaches its conclusion, the final mood is not one of surging aspiration to the ideal, but of veiled hope for a more subdued authority. The prophet is not a man who knows only the intellectual wonders of heaven, but studies rather the facts observed while tied to earth:

> And may at last my weary age
> Find out the peaceful hermitage,
> The Hairy Gown and Mossy Cell,
> Where I may sit and rightly spell

Of every Star that Heav'n doth shew
And every Herb that sips the dew,
Till old experience do attain
To something like Prophetic strain.

In terms of the tension between Eros and Agape as
defined by Nygren, *Il Penseroso* marks a strong shift
towards the rhythms of Agape and away from the
escapism of *L'Allegro*, which presents a world devoid
of any fully recognized sin, failure, and ugliness. If the
games theory of *L'Allegro* is not quite Platonic either,
it still comes close to admiration of the self-sufficient
virtuosity which is one attractive factor for intellectuals
in the Socratic dialectic. Practical efficiency has never
been Platonism's strong point despite the idea of the
Republic's dependence on highly trained guardians.
Plato's own failure in Syracuse, and the total indiffer-
ence to worldly affairs of Plotinus are quite representative of the tradition. Modern variants can be seen
in men like Ficino, Henry More, or Spinoza: subtle
personalities all, but marginal to the great events of
the day—unlike practically committed Christians such
as Cromwell, Newton, or Pascal, who show astounding
efficiency in worldly matters, whether bureaucratic or
scientific.

Milton is once again illustrating an instinctive movement toward the pragmatic and away from metaphysics.
The mastery of his "prophet" has something practical
and yet intuitive about it: he is inspired and observant,
but not confident or systematic. The ambiguous words
"rightly spell" may suggest struggling simplicity rather
than suave virtuosity. But the type of knowledge involved remains impersonal, non-human. Milton notably

fails to achieve any sense of the integration of this practical wisdom with an existing human community. The satisfactions of his prophet remain private and egotistical, in a word, inhumane. The young poet is not yet able to escape from a selfish kind of intellectual satisfaction whose practical value is questionable.

However, the personal characterization of the speaker is stronger and more consistent than that in the poems discussed earlier, and this marks a step toward the richness of baroque art at its best in which the artist's own role is realistically and vividly expressed, as in Velasquez' famous painting of himself and the young princess with her attendants, or in Rembrandt's self-portraits. The important point is not that *L'Allegro* and *Il Penseroso* are fully autobiographical, but that their speaker (like that of Shakespeare's *Sonnets*) cannot be shown in any specific way to be incompatible with their historical author. This plausibility gives them a local color, a piquant flavor of authenticity which has always been a feature of popular art, however suspect this mundane realism may be to idealizing aestheticians. Other things being equal in artistic endeavor, a vividly documentary aspect has always been a positive attribute for the general audience, as the continued popularity of Rubens and Rembrandt seems to confirm.

Comus

This immediacy of the twin elegies provides a perfect corollary with Milton's interest in the masque form. As Stephen Orgel has so deftly shown in his study of Jonson,[4] the masque differs from drama in general

---

[4] S. Orgel, *The Jonsonian Masque* (Cambridge: Harvard University Press, 1965)

precisely because it is a supremely occasional form: no
revival can ever recover the relevance of a masque to
the original event which it celebrated. Most masques
reach their climaxes by directly impinging on the personalities of their first audience, usually the guests and
principals at some state event or symbolic festivity.
"Arcades" is perhaps too slight and innocently compli-
mentary to illustrate these attributes fully, despite the
attractions of its Spenserian musicality. But the impact
of *Comus* cannot be grasped fully unless its documentary
qualities are established. At first sight it is a rather stiff
allegory in which frigid virtue, with the aid of various
intellectual powers, escapes libidinous assault. In these
terms, it has always seemed to most scholars and critics
to be largely Platonic in theme, texture, and characterization. All the virtuous characters have a kind of
smug, not to say supercilious, self-confidence. The opening speech of the Attendant Spirit seems to set the tone.
He lives:

> where those immortal shapes
> Of bright aërial Spirits live inspher'd
> In Regions mild of calm and serene Air,
> Above the smoke and stir of this dim spot
> Which men call Earth, and, with low-thoughted care,
> Confin'd and pestered in this pinfold here,
> Strive to keep up a frail and Feverish being,
> Unmindful of the crown that Virtue gives
> After this mortal change, to her true Servants
> Amongst the enthron'd gods on Sainted seats.
> Yet some there be that by due steps aspire
> To lay their just hands on that Golden Key
> That opes the Palace of Eternity.

(2-14)

Here Milton establishes that the "world" of his masque ensures merit's reward, an initial position exactly opposed to the puritan ideas of predestination and unmerited grace. The value of rectitude and works as preparatory for grace was stressed by the opponents of the puritans, not only by Anglicans like Hooker, but by Jesuits like Molina, whose views (though unusually melioristic) perhaps explain why the Jesuits also laid so much stress on education and systematic training. Coupled with such a positive and premeditated pursuit of virtue there tends to go its more obviously pernicious corollary: a too-relentless hatred of vice, which because it must be premeditated also is, therefore, doubly detestable. The severity of judgment passed against the sensual Comus by all the virtuous characters in the masque matches well with the latent schizophrenia of Platonism, which tends to cut up human nature into two halves (like Socrates' two horses)—isolating intellect and spirit from the senses and the body.

The two brothers in the masque achieve almost a caricature of this system. If self-conscious merit is properly rewarded as they believe, then virtue can never truly be harmed even in body; and this argument produces a clearly magical approach to chastity, which in its ideal form is conceived to have compelling powers not only to tame evil but to exact support from the gods:

> She has a hidden strength . . .
> 'Tis chastity, my brother, chastity:
> She that has that is clad in complete steel . . .
> No savage fierce, Bandit or mountaineer,
> Will dare to soil her Virgin purity. . . .
> Some say no evil thing that walks by night . . .

No goblin or swart Faëry of the mine,
Hath hurtful power o'er true virginity.
Do ye believe me yet, or shall I call
Antiquity from the old Schools of *Greece*
To testify the arms of Chastity? . . .
So dear to ·Heav'n is Saintly chastity
That when a soul is found sincerely so,
A thousand liveried Angles lackey her,
Driving far off each thing of sin and guilt,
And in clear dream and solemn vision
Tell her of things that no gross ear can hear,
Till oft converse with heav'nly habitants
Begin to cast a beam on th'outward shape,
The unpolluted temple of the mind,
And turns it by degrees to the soul's essence,
Till all be made immortal.
      (415, 420-421, 426-427, 432, 437-440, 453-463)

Some scholars have assumed these naively idealistic
views to be exactly Milton's own, but even a youthful
Milton was not quite so simple as to accept this sentimental recension of Plato's transcendence of sexuality
in the *Symposium*. Only a few lines earlier, the masque
had shown how exactly wrong the elder brother's analysis could be: far from being isolated from vice by her
virtue, it is precisely her naive lack of experience of evil
that allows the Lady to be immobilized by Comus.
There cannot be any doubt of Milton's dramatic irony
when the younger brother cheerfully forgets his sister's
fate to paraphrase Plato (*Republic*, Bk. VI, 487-489):

How charming is divine Philosophy!
Not harsh and crabbed as dull fools suppose,
But musical as is *Apollo's* lute.
      (476-478)

Obviously an uncritical acceptance of the views of the virtuous and innocent characters in the masque as Milton's own is a shallow response invalidated by the action and indeed also by associations like the comparable naiveté of Shakespeare's doomed Richard II in similar circumstances:

God for his Richard hath in heavenly pay
A glorious angel: then, if angels fight,
Weak men must fall, for heaven still guards the right.
(III.ii.60-62)

The best way to escape from a naive misreading of *Comus* is to rethink our responses to the piece, seeing it specifically as a masque, not as subjective lyric verse— that is, we must seek to view it in its historical context, as an expression of immediate facts and practical implications. That Milton thought of this masque as a function of a particular time and place and not simply as an abstract moral drama is easy to demonstrate. It is true that it finds literary antecedents which lie in much earlier works of Jonson—a sequence of two masques called *Pleasure Reconciled with Virtue* and *A Prospect of Wales*—but these also focus on a specific occasion: the first participation in a masque of the future Charles I, in his role of Prince of Wales which makes him officially heir to the throne of England. The first of the Jonson masques for this occasion deals with a practical and immediate issue: the nature of authority's relation to indulgence and relaxation, a topic that proved of major interest to Milton. This first masque also introduces Comus as a figure associated with indulgence. It shows symbolically that pleasurable relaxation is not of itself unfit: for example, after his labors Hercules may properly enjoy himself. The second masque rephrases the discussion of Charles' role in more explicit terms, stressing the truly civilized and positive qualities of the royal heir's principality of Wales, which the English traditionally regarded as primitive and barbarous as we see throughout Shakespeare's *Henry IV, Part I*. This focus on the threatening aspect of Wales is obviously what triggers Milton's association of these Jonson masques with the elevation of the Earl of Bridgewater to the rank of Lord President of Wales, which is the actual event *Comus* celebrates in its turn.

Jonson and Milton are thus both counseling aristocrats of high rank on their roles in handling an alien, subtle, and potentially threatening community. It is not quite fair to say that Milton equates the "druidic" or "Celtic" traditions of Welsh culture with the sinister magic of Circe and Comus, but the two ancient traditions are seen as somewhat comparable—at least as non-English. Milton also cleverly exploits another circumstantial aspect of his masque's initial and definitive moment of performance: that it was to be presented on Michaelmas Eve. This significant seasonal setting allows Milton to extend his discussion of the role of good government to apply to all societies which have to regulate the annual excess of harvest time with its tradition of orgiastic festivals. *Comus* is thus in sense a "harvest masque" closely comparable to "the masque of Ceres" in *The Tempest* which serves to admonish Ferdinand and Miranda about the misuse of fertility in relation to their impending marriage. *Comus* confronts the risk of diabolic misuse of the harvest's prodigality with the contrasting festival spirit of St. Michael, who traditionally overthrows Satan in the War in Heaven. The defeat of Comus thus has an archetype of a very precise kind.

However, Milton balances this broader issue by investing his masque with many local allusions to Bridgewater's territorial role as a protector of the Welsh-English frontier roughly marked by the basin of the River Severn—a river whose tutelary spirit is the Lady's rescuer, Sabrina. Ludlow, where the masque was first performed, lies close to this river. Milton's casting of the roles enhances this particularity of reference, for he has the Bridgewater children play themselves with sufficient realism for the central episode of their straying and being separated in the woods to provoke a local legend in Ludlow that it was an actual occurrence (as Oldys and Masson have both recorded, though the masque's plot seems in part to be borrowed from an ancient folkstory). Moreover, the guardian spirit's role is also typecast, being played by the children's music tutor, Henry Lawes, whose speeches often closely fit his actual role in the family.

There is a further advantage in the children's prominence in the masque; for while the aging Ben Jonson might properly advise the youthful Prince of Wales about his demeanor as ruler, the youthful Milton could scarcely presume to admonish the mature and experienced Earl of Bridgewater. In presenting the children's well-intentioned but inexpert characters, Milton could draw to the Earl's attention the errors of naive virtue and implicitly warn him of their bearing on his role both as father, and as governor of a province. If this diagnosis of the masque's purpose is correct, then our response to its Platonic elements must be much modified; and in corroboration we shall find some of its puzzling attributes resolved. For example, there has been unfavorable comment on the Lady's priggishness, and scholarly censure of the popular title of *Comus* now firmly fixed on the originally nameless masque. The popular choice of title reflects the bizarre fact that Comus is the most vivacious and convincing character in the masque, and this would seem to suggest a false emphasis if the suposed intent of the masque was to flatter the Earl by making his daughter the perfect heroine, and her brothers models of intelligent rectitude.

However, the basic purpose of a Jonsonian masque was never merely to flatter or divert, but rather to use these approaches to instruct—or at least make virtues visible by ascription of them to his audience, whether or not they actually possessed them. The children's failures are quite unmistakable, if perfectly innocent, deriving essentially from the conviction that virtue is a passive and self-sufficient good (they share the kind of complacency which causes Shakespeare's youthful Richard II to lose his throne to the wily Bolinbroke). The Lady is too confident and the harshness of her rejection of self-indulgence is perhaps deliberately over-censorious in tone. The point of the masque lies in its demonstration that mere rectitude can only arrive at a stalemate with vice. The Lady's will may reject Comus' blandishment but her body acknowledges his authority up to a point. Her paralysis might even be described in modern psychiatric terms as a neurotic dysfunction resulting from fear of repressed sensuality. Frightened that her body may involuntarily respond to the promptings of the libido, the superego of the Lady can find temporary safety only in rejecting *every* movement.

This situation is obviously not satisfactory, for it leaves us with a sense of the Lady's insufficiency to overcome her trials. The implicit admonition to the Earl of Bridgewater is also clear: he will not dominate the alien Welsh simply by self-confident rectitude. Nor will ambitious reasoning, such as the brothers employ, help: alone they are powerless, and they also even manage to wreck the victory over Comus at the end. Even their angelic attendant spirit cannot himself achieve a decisive action. Only Sabrina can accomplish the liberation of the Lady, and her significance seems extraordinarily elusive to modern scholars. Although the climactic action of the play establishes Sabrina as the power who turns the balance in favor of virtue, the derivation of that power remains uncertain. She is not intelligible to moderns as a function of human intelligence, and she is not to be commanded by any institutional ritual, though her response to prayer is gracious. Perhaps this enigmatic figure will become more intelligible if we can accumulate the circumstantial detail with which the name of Sabrina was invested for Milton and for the inhabitants of the valley of the Severn.

Sabrina originally appears in a pathetic role in the ancient and celebrated story of Locrine, who was forced to abandon his beloved to marry an unsympathetic woman. Renewing his relationship with his preferred mistress, Locrine made her pregnant and Sabrina was born of the loving but adulterous union. The discovery of this provoked the fury of Locrine's legal wife, who took revenge by the brutal murder both of her rival and of the illegitimate love-child. Sabrina's body was cast into the Severn, which supposedly takes its current name from a corruption of the name of the innocent victim who became its tutelary deity. The story has always been popular in England, probably for its blend of pathos, sentiment, and savagery. It was exploited in a flamboyant sixteenth-century tragedy, as well as in *The Mirror for Magistrates*, so that Sabrina would be doubly familiar to an educated aristocrat living on the banks of the Severn. The juxtaposition of Sabrina, as apotheosis of this pathetic little murdered bastard, with the snobbish and pompous Lady, and the dominant role this pathetic victim has at the climactic moment in *Comus*, both require us to establish Sabrina's exact relation to the other figures. First, as a murdered infant she is both innocent and yet also a total disproof of the view that innocence will be somehow protected. Her adulterous origin relates her to the libidinous forces epitomized by Comus, yet these blemishes themselves result not from any gross crime on her part or her parents' but from the wrenching forces of political circumstance. Lastly the powers of affronted "virtue" as displayed in Locrine's embittered wife are the ones ultimately guilty of the most vicious acts in the whole story.

Thus the reincarnated Sabrina is uniquely qualified to arbitrate between the forces of good and evil. Moreover, as the spirit of the Severn she shares the role of the Earl of Bridgewater as a Lord of the Marches, for the Severn verges on the traditional boundary between England and Wales. The valley of the Severn partakes of both cultures, and its sinuosities provide a flexible symbol for the subtle interpenetration of forces which must take place both in a truly United Kingdom, and also in any discriminating articulation of the relations between good and evil in the individual, the family, or larger groups. With its fluidity and fertilizing qualities, water is itself an ideal symbol for creativity, flexibility, and subtleness. There is nothing rigid about Sabrina, and her spirit can thaw the Lady out of her catatonic trance by helping to minimize the tensions provoked by the sinister attractions of Comus. That water is traditionally associated with baptism for Milton's Christian audience merely confirms how suitable it is as a symbol for resolving the tensions of sin and restoring a clean and vigorous state of mind. For Sabrina is not merely a ritual symbol.

The main point of Sabrina's role must surely lie in the superior power of her subtle effectiveness to that of the Lady's obtuse and rigid virtue. Milton thereby warns his audience against elementary moral views of the self-sufficiency of rectitude, and reminds them that even horror may generate sweetness and strength. Stiff and rigorous excellence is not enough for ultimate success, the origins of which often prove unpredictably paradoxical as in Sabrina's case. The Earl will be well advised to take Sabrina as his model in regulating both his family and his governorship, bearing in mind that often his subtlest policies will be garbled by such innocent incompetence as that of the brothers, who in their eagerness allow the evil spirit of Comus to escape and thus, appropriately, to remain free to cause further troubles. The war with such disruptive powers is unlikely to be ended neatly in total victory, and even temporary advantage can only be won by an almost superhuman suppleness born out of the involuntary experience of suffering. If we wish to be doctrinaire, we may christen this unpredictable and spontaneously acquired resource grace, but its name hardly matters and Milton does not stress this terminology.

If my explication of the masque's tenor is correct, it follows that it illustrates strikingly the Diffusionist pattern of intellectual evolution mentioned earlier.[5] The traditional critic's view of the masque is that it is merely a rather abstract, idealistic allegory in which virtue is vindicated—the kind of morality play that has frequently recurred among Western intellectuals since the *Psychomachia* of Prudentius. To the extent that this is true (and it may partly account for the masque's lack of impact) it indicates the pernicious literary effect of overintellectuality, which schematizes characters and issues, polarizes values and efficiency, and reduces the full literary spectrum to a severe, silvery chiaroscuro. But if creativity is the result of a unique interaction of historical circumstances, and these are uncovered and brought to bear on a work like *Comus*, it may elude conventional valuation and recover its rich distinctiveness. For example, we have found a means to accommodate the immaturity of the Lady and her brothers, and to rationalize the role of Sabrina. If Milton as poet was not so naively impressed with an immature idealism as he has been thought to be in his prose, the power and charm of Comus are more likely to be deliberate and his role may rightly merit the predominance assigned by the masque's modern name, for then the whole point would be to stress how powerful Comus is, not to celebrate his easy defeat by even inept youths.

My claims for the masque depend absolutely on the way its uniqueness derives from its context, but there remains some discrepancy between Milton's awareness of what he is intuitively accomplishing, and the more

[5] See p 21.

deliberate parts of his art. Despite the unmistakable
point of his plot structure, he becomes too involved in
ratiocinative dialogue, and the result is often a stiff
texture at variance with the provocativeness of his most
basic intuitions. Like Hamlet, the youthful Milton is
always lapsing into antique orthodoxy. While Hamlet
is inclined to revert to the non-Christian cult of the
lex talonis advocated by his father's ghost, Milton
cannot consciously purge himself of a deeply conditioned
attraction to the more or less Platonic ethic deriving
from his reading and intellectual environment. Thus,
having shown that the paralysis of rigid ethics can only
be dissolved by a sinuous flexibility of truly ominous
derivation, Milton allows the masque to relapse into
naive ideology at its conclusion, an ideology reduced
to facile confidence by the attendant Spirit's dogmatic
assertion:

> Mortals that would follow me,
> Love virtue, she alone is free,
> She can teach ye how to climb
> Higher than the Sphery chime;
> Or if Virtue feeble were,
> Heav'n itself would stoop to her.

> (1018-1023)

This idea that virtue is self-sufficient for salvation, or
even the secondary assertion that God will protect the
just, are views which the plot has questioned and all
experience disproves—as the mature Milton recognizes
gloomily via the chorus of *Samson Agonistes* (652-704).
However, at the time *Comus* was written the young poet
may have decided that he should not present too Calvinistic a sense of the futility of deliberate virtue in a

brusque and open way while addressing the household
of a major royal official and magistrate.

Lycidas

Whatever the reason for Milton's avoidance of overt
puritanism in *Comus*, we see that this balance of stilted
orthodoxy and subjective awareness is brusquely re-
versed in *Lycidas*. Where idealistic theorizing had previously deadened gleams of nonconformity, now the
picturesque rags of neoclassical pastoralism scarcely
serve to conceal the stout Pauline armour of puritan
fervor confidently assumed by the poet. His nominally
equivocal posture in *Comus*, and his intellectual detachment in the elegies, are now brusquely cast off under
the impact of his subjective anxieties and resentments.
Yet even so, these stresses derive more from a fear of
missing conventional success than from revolutionary
fervor. *Lycidas* is a desperate attempt to find orthodox
reasons for accepting that conscious virtue may fail to
secure its merited reward. The reasons Milton offers for
accepting the threat of premature death presented by
King's drowning are orthodox, but they are more Christian than Platonic. The verdict on man's efforts is not
made through his conscious sense of the attainment of
his own overt goals, but via God's omniscient and
mysterious verdict, based on standards beyond worldly
knowledge. Only a tiny shift of phrasing is needed to
turn this view into a repudiation of the doctrine of merit:
if God's "perfect witness" fully eludes human judgment,
redemption becomes unpredictable, as the puritans
maintained. Classical "virtue" becomes irrelevant, and

humble failure becomes as likely to be the occasion of salvation as kingly achievement. Certainly the showy manners of Laud's visible church are no longer proof of virtue; its "lean and flashy songs" are not even signs of substantial worth. The redemption of King-Lycidas has nothing to do with either his status or his achievements:

> So *Lycidas*, sunk low, but mounted high,
> Through the dear might of him that walk'd the waves.

What has given the poem its real bite is not the elegant mosaic of pretty fragments lifted from the pastoral tradition but its sharp edge of personal anxiety and bitterness painfully sheathed only after the recognition of the inadequacy of conventional victory as a goal. But this sense of inadequacy is born in the poet less as a result of deliberate or even spontaneous insight than of an increasing fear of actual failure in himself. The awareness derives from unique historical circumstances like King's death (and even the threat of the raging plague of the period) and their implications for a young man who is himself setting out on an uncertain and perilous journey which will remove him from the immediate competition for national honors. Thus we find that the core of one of Milton's most famous poems is not the result of the calculated art for which it is conventionally praised, but rather the painful product of external circumstances to which the poet reluctantly has to accommodate himself. *Lycidas* is one of the last major pastoral poems of the Renaissance, notable less for its author's conventional mastery of an archaic pastoral tradition than for its resentfully modern recognition of unpalatable experience. The dramatic virtue of the poem lies primarily in convincingly assimilating the possibility of failure, to the point that the author (or his poetic persona) can plausibly continue on his life's risky journey with some firmness: "Tomorrow to fresh Woods, and Pastures new."

I have already asserted that this truly heroic rhythm of ambitious failure succeeded by calm resolve is Milton's unique contribution to Western tradition. Of no other author in the European tradition, not even Dante, is this pattern so characteristic, and in no other corpus of poetry is it so vividly documented and deliberately explored by the author as when Milton comes to understand his experiences. But while *Lycidas* may seem to be his most sustained youthful statement of the cycle, it contains many dead patches of suave yet mechanical pastoralism, as anyone who tries to read it to a general audience painfully discovers. All those lists of plants and flowers too obviously borrow from a moribund georgic tradition. I have found that for a modern audience the most effective display of Milton's maturing powers seems to lie elsewhere—in his mastery of another traditional but dying genre for which his mastery provides a powerful coda: the sonnet sequence.

The Sonnets

It is not accidental that Milton's sonnets became so important for the Romantic and Victorian poets. Far more than Donne's poems do, these sonnets anticipate the harsh tones of modern lyricism, as Wordsworth so vehemently stressed:

Milton! thou shouldst be living at this hour:
England hath need of thee: she is a fen
Of stagnant waters: altar, sword, and pen,
Fireside, the heroic wealth of hall and bower,
Have forfeited their ancient English dower
Of inward happiness. We are selfish men;
Oh! raise us up, return to us again;
And give us manners, virtue, freedom, power.
Thy soul was like a Star, and dwelt apart;
Thou hadst a voice whose sound was like the sea:
Pure as the naked heavens, majestic, free,
So didst thou travel on life's common way,
In cheerful godliness; and yet thy heart
The lowliest duties on herself did lay.[6]

The qualities stressed here are not those associated with earlier sonnet cycles in English like those of Spenser and Sidney, where a conventional Platonic sensibility had struggled to stifle sexuality and common sense. The saturation in idealized subjectivity, with which such cycles are associated, illustrates both the egotism and the obtuseness to which the Platonic aspiration deflects the literary imagination. It is no accident that the greatest sonneteers, Petrarch, Ronsard, Wyatt, Shakespeare, or Donne, vindicate their creativity by definitively rejecting the seductive affectations of sentimental idealization of their mistresses as they reach emotional and poetic maturity, so that their most powerful sonnets are often disillusioned not to say sardonic in tone, like Shakespeare's 130 or 138.

[6] W. Wordsworth, *The Poetical Works*, edited by Ernest de Selincourt (Oxford: Oxford University Press, 1904), p. 307.

Inheriting this tradition, Milton was largely spared
the obligation to work his way slowly toward the inevitable reversal of values which the sentimental tradition
exacted of poets who sought to transcend affected ecstasy. Indeed one might claim that only one English
sonnet of Milton recalls the extinct posturing phase of
the cycles, his first. And even in it the invocation of
the conventional nightingale proves as fallacious as the
expectation of its song in *Il Penseroso*: expecting the
good amatory omen in vain, Milton's speaker (little
different from himself, it would seem) has to reconcile
himself to the fact that his sentimental life is nonexis-
tent. This practical disadvantage starts the sonnets off
deliberately on a false note with the ominous cry of
the cuckoo.

It seems possible to an editor like E. A. J. Honigman
that Milton intended the sonnets to be read as a
sequence, for we know that over the years he deliberately rearranges the sonnets, breaking their chrono-
logical order as if experimenting to find evolving cycles
of experience. The two first English sonnets were
written well before the other English ones, as confirmed
chronologically by the second one which laments his
lack of creativity before his "three and twentieth year."
Milton divides this one from the first poem by inserting
the five more sentimental Italian sonnets supposedly
celebrating an Italian lady. The intrusion of Italian style
and sentiments might seem accidental, but editors agree
that Milton wanted exactly this sequence; the reason
is obvious if we consider the dramatic plausibility in
the evolving pattern of the opening sonnets. First a
lonely young man wishes he was in love; then, with

his wish granted, he sentimentally courts an alien beauty in a stilted and unfamiliar language, only to wake with a shock to find that (at twenty-three) his youth is passing and he has nothing to show for it. Indeed, by the eighth sonnet he finds he must try to defend himself from the threat of death at the hands of the royalist armies that are advancing on his home in London. Such are the rewards of high sentiment: alien philandering, uncreativity, and abrupt assault by hostile forces. The pattern is quite corroborative of what we saw in *Comus*, but there is a more mature attitude seen in the early acceptance of failure if that is God's will, which appears as soon as the sonnet about being twenty-three.

After this sentimental series, Milton shows us reality breaking in, first with the royalist threat, and then in two sonnets in which women are not treated as the excuse for sentimental persiflage but as real people with worthwhile values, functions, and identities comparable to the poet's own. The first young lady is praised because she,

> Wisely hast shunn'd the broad way and the green,
> And with those few art eminently seen
> That labour up the Hill of Heav'nly Truth.

Perhaps this still verges on conventional idealization, but the calculated prosaicisms of the next sonnet are intended to show how far the poet has repudiated suave Petrarchanism:

> Daughter to that good Earl, once President
>   Of *England's* Council and her Treasury, . . .
> Though later born than to have known the days

> Wherein your Father flourisht, yet by you,
>   Madam, methinks I see him living yet;
> So well your words his noble virtues praise
>   That all both judge you to relate them true
>   And to possess them, Honor'd *Margaret.*

The sonnet marks a surprising revival of the blunt moralizing style in which Jonson excelled. But Milton can show more colloquial virtuosity than this, as his next sonnet proves. Here there is a sense of historical particularity blended with a dramatic vigor akin to Donne's:

> A book was writ of late call'd *Tetrachordon*;
>   And wov'n close, both matter, form and style;
>   The Subject new: it walk'd the Town a while
>   Numb'ring good intellects; now seldom por'd on.
> Cries the stall-reader, "Bless us! what a word on
>   A title-page is this!" and some in file
>   Stand spelling false, while one might walk to Mile-
>   End Green.

The brusque, sardonic style is as distinctive as the subject itself in the sonnet cycles of the English Renaissance, and they mark so polemical a view of the sonnet form that the poem had to wait a hundred and fifty years before Romantics like Wordsworth were able to match such a lively model. For Milton, as with Petrarch denouncing the Papal Court at Avignon, the sonnet has ceased to be a sentimental exercise and has become the poetic equivalent of a sawn-off shotgun with which to blast one's enemies' morale. This function is even more vigorously achieved in the enlarged sonnet entitled: "On the New Forcers of Conscience under the Long Parliament" which would have struck the intransigent Presbyterians in Parliament like a whiff of grapeshot, followed by the *coup de grâce* of its last line: "New Presbyter is but old Priest writ large."

These poems of calculated polemical violence are not the high point of the sequence. They represent in their context as a whole only a partial advance to full maturity. If Milton's poetry is now muscular enough to handle contemporary social and political issues directly, the impulse governing this verse remains idealistic. Even the contempt for democracy is a traditional corollary of Platonic attitudes in *The Republic* (VIII, 557-558), for Milton wrote in his other sonnet on *Tetrachordon*:

> this is got by casting Pearl to Hogs,
> That bawl for freedom in their senseless mood,
> And still revolt when truth would set them free.
> License they mean when they cry liberty;
> For who loves that, must first be wise and good.

The argument here is exactly that attacked by St. Augustine when it was advanced by Pelagius and the Donatists: that merit is a proper prerequisite of legitimacy. All history seems to show the reverse of this Aristotelian view, since power as often redeems the unworthy as it corrupts the virtuous, despite Acton's axiom to the contrary. Thus the stridency of Milton's resentment against those who censured his pamphlets is just as much a function of sentimental idealism as were the sexual sublimations of the neo-Petrarchan sonneteers. The sonnet form does not reach its climax in them for they miss the full range of poetic and psychological awareness.

And indeed these polemics are followed by a series of sonnets that are surprisingly subdued. After trying to blast the Presbyterians out of Parliament, we find Milton abruptly recognizing the virtue of a very different kind of style, that of Henry Lawes:

> whose tuneful and well-measur'd Song
> First taught our English Music how to span
> Words with just note and accent.

This more measured tone reappears in Milton's praise "of Mrs. Catharine Thomson, my Christian Friend, Deceased." Her virtues were private, and the sonnet steadily insists on their dependence upon the "Faith and Love" of their possessor rather than on any idealistic ambition to excel. The vindicated but private worth of Mrs. Thomson seems superior to that seen in Milton's subsequent admonitions to the two great leaders of the Parliamentary forces, both of whom are warned that their proven virtues have not been adequate for the redemption of England. General Fairfax is told: "In vain doth Valor bleed / While Avarice and Rapine share the land." Cromwell's victories are equally undercut:

> yet much remains
> To conquer still; peace hath her victories
> No less renowned than war, new foes arise.

Virtue seems less and less all-sufficient: only the gifts of a Harry Vane are praised without reserve in a sonnet, and these are of the contemplative rather than the active order. They are more those of understanding and knowledge than of command. Milton's sense that great accomplishment is easily attained by heroic minds has begun to recede.

We come next without surprise to the first truly tragic sonnet: "On the Late Massacre in Piemont." The true reward of virtue is seen frankly for the first time in Milton's verse, and he admits what he dared not recognize in "The Passion" and failed to make explicit in *Comus*: that human justice is impotent before the wrongs of the world:

> Avenge, O Lord, thy slaughter'd Saints, whose bones
>> Lie scatter'd on the Alpine mountains cold,
>> Ev'n them who kept thy truth so pure of old
>> When all our Fathers worship't Stocks and Stones,
> Forget not: in thy book record their groans
>> Who were thy Sheep and in their ancient Fold
>> Slain by the bloody *Piemontese*, that roll'd
>> Mother with Infant down the Rocks.

In *Lycidas* Milton had faced the fact that worth might not guarantee success, and had deplored the superficiality of Laudian Christianity. But now he has to face the fact of the mass murder of Christians whose virtues he deeply admires. The veiled fate of the mythical Sabrina suddenly finds an immediate modern equivalent. The shock to Milton's confidence in human reason is obviously immense: he is reduced to shouting at God, "Do something about it, for heaven's sake!"

Of course, it is quite typical of Milton even at this late stage to give God the benefit of his advice—indeed, of a few brisk orders so that He may keep His books straight. Milton has certainly escaped from the Platonic ecstasy, but he has not got as far as the New Testament, yet. Rather he is stuck somewhere back among the more resentful Old Testament prophets, say with Amos—or more relevantly perhaps one might suggest Jonah, for

Milton is about to be swallowed up by a darkness from which he will be spewed out into a new light different from any he had ever seen, whose dawning is deliberately commemorated in the last five sonnets of the series. They are in their way the nearest thing to an expression of true wisdom that Milton ever wrote.

The sonnet "On his Blindness" copes with a more severe sense of failure than that written in his twenty-third year. Milton is older, and he has sacrificed his prime to inferior if idealistic aims—aims which he has even so failed to accomplish, while seemingly losing through blindness the possibility of recouping his inadequacy. Yet the tone of the sonnet is never hopeless. Nor is the conclusion quite as passive as it is usually considered to be. "They also serve who only stand and wait" implies two kinds of positive virtue which Milton comes to see as the *only* kinds of virtue, even though they contrast with both the strenuously idealistic aspirations of his early years and the political activism which governed his service to the Commonwealth. The minimal virtue of standing still (apart from the tremendous self-discipline it requires) is that it does not do positive harm. After the tumult and violence of civil war, Milton is becoming less impressed with the mere physical facts of victory, as his sonnets to Fairfax and Cromwell clearly show. He is no longer impressed by those "That bawl for freedom in their senseless mood," and is positively hostile to the energetic errors of the "reforming" Presbyterians. Milton now seems to recognize by mere necessity that inactivity and patience may be the signs of greater insight and authority than ostentatious commitment and violent action.

The second phase of virtue lies in the consequence of this first one: those who "stand and wait" by implication wait *for* something. The sonnet cannot yet predict what this outcome may be for Milton, and only with his two last works, *Paradise Regained* and *Samson Agonistes*, was Milton able to display fully the psychology of his new heroic ideal and its translation into drastic action. However, as early as the sonnet about blindness he rejects the idea of rational prediction in favor of something we might call an existential imperative, but which Christians have tended to identify as the Will of God, and which encourages them to do the most unpredictable things. As a way of founding a world religion, for example, getting oneself executed like a common criminal seems pretty silly, but has in fact proved far more effective as a way of stabilizing society than the world conquests of an Alexander or even an Augustus—let alone the legalistic labors of a Justinian or the enlightened despotism of a Louis XIV or a Napoleon.

Milton's sonnet on his blindness is thus the turning point in his career both as a thinker and as a poet. It includes both an absolute rejection of the restless pursuit of perfection (the most impressive aspect of the Platonic tradition) and the acceptance of an incompetence which is the opposite of the supercilious sense of his own merit, to which the more complacent intellectual is so prone. With these attitudes goes a whole change in his life style. It is probably not accidental that Milton places next to this sonnet of serene acceptance of the defeat of his ambitions the most civilized and urbane of all his poems—a poem in which hearty good sense and simple enjoyment of life's pleasures are delightfully expressed. Anyone considering the stridency of some of Milton's previous writing should recognize that the triumphs of his later years are better understood if we start from this almost Epicurean statement of his recovered delight in domestic satisfactions. Horace never put it better:

> Lawrence of virtuous Father virtuous Son,
>> Now that the Fields are dank and ways are mire,
>> Where shall we sometimes meet and by the fire
>> Help waste a sullen day, what may be won
> From the hard Season gaining? Time will run
>> On smoother, till *Favonius* re-inspire
>> The frozen earth, and clothe in fresh attire
>> The Lily and Rose, that neither sow'd nor spun.
> What neat repast shall feast us, light and choice,
>> Of Attic taste, with Wine, whence we may rise
>> To hear the Lute well touched, or artful voice
> Warble immortal Notes and *Tuscan* Air?
>> He who of those delights can judge and spare
>> To interpose them oft, is not unwise.

Any simple hostility to Milton as a soured puritan can surely not survive this suave and subtle reconciliation to adverse circumstances. One should note that there is no escapist hedonism here but rather the sense that the power to enjoy life is a mark of psychological health, indeed of religious virtue. For the allusion to the parable of the lily of the field reminds us that Christ favored the relaxed attention of Mary over the fussy officiousness of Martha. In other words, there is more to Milton's cheerful domesticity than Epicurean agnosticism. It becomes an expression of readiness to respond positively to anything that life brings, however humble, and this readiness is the psychological point at which true urbanity and the original spirit of Christianity intersect. After all, for his first miracle Christ did change water to wine when supplies ran out at the wedding-party in Cana.

The sonnet to Cyriak Skinner shows how far Milton has come from "the hydroptic thirst after knowledge" displayed in *Of Education*. If his sonnet to Lawrence expresses surprising satisfaction in the simple, sensuous pleasures of ordinary life, the Cyriak one shows contempt for pedantic relentlessness:

> Today deep thoughts resolve with me to drench
>   In mirth, that after no repenting draws;
>   Let *Euclid* rest and *Archimedes* pause,
>   And what the *Swede* intend, and what the *French*.
> To measure life learn thou betimes, and know
>   Toward solid good what leads the nearest way;
>   For other things mild Heav'n a time ordains,
> And disapproves that care, though wise in show,
>   That with superfluous burden loads the day,
>   And, when God sends a cheerful hour, refrains.

The earlier lines have an almost Falstaffian ring about them—indeed the whole poem might be mistaken for a mere rationalization of indolence if we did not know its author for one of the most strenuous and disciplined of men. For this contextual reason we should look at the poem closely; it fully resolves the problem posed in *Comus*: the relation of conscious virtue to relaxation.

The answer was implicit in the Lady's neurotic tension: true maturity best shows itself by a flexible response to experience. Unremitting effort is deadly to real insight, creativity, and effort. Leonard Woolf has summed up the issue well in the third volume of his autobiography by insisting "upon the importance of bouts of idleness and of not thinking, for creative thought. Nearly everyone must have had the experience of grinding away at some intellectual or even emotional problem and than suddenly, when one has given it up in desperation and is thinking of something entirely different, the solution comes with a flash, 'like an inspiration,' into the mind. Or you may even go to bed with an unsolved problem and wake next morning to find you have solved it in sleep. The most famous example of this phenomenon is the triumphant 'Eureka' of Archimedes when he leapt from his bath, having seen in a sudden flash the scientific principle which had so long eluded him in his study."[7] It is curious that Woolf should have fallen on the same illustration as Milton, and his comment makes us reread Milton's line more meaningfully: "Let *Euclid* rest, and *Archimedes* pause."

There is an unconscious hint of irony in the penultimate sonnet of the cycle, also addressed to Cyriack Skinner, for it contradicts the previous one and relapses into complacency over Milton's loss of sight from his eyes:

> What supports me, dost thou ask?
> The conscience, Friend, to have lost them overplied
> In liberty's defence, my noble task,
> Of which all Europe talks from side to side.

If this had been the last of the sonnets known, we might well feel Milton's evolution in the form was from naive ambition to megalomania. But we should note the

[7]Leonard Woolf, *Beginning Again* (London: Hogarth Press, 1964), p. 32.

implication (however involuntary) of the phrase "to have lost them overplied / In liberty's defence." The word "overplied" resonates interestingly with the reproach against the man "that with superfluous burden loads the day" and allows himself no respite from "deep thoughts."

We know that Milton did not abandon the sonnet form and the theme of his blindness in this mood of unhistorical confidence in his triumphs: after all, that sonnet itself could not be published because its complacency ran counter to the facts of the Restoration, and of Milton's consequent humiliation. It is thus appropriate historically, chronologically, and aesthetically that the cycle close with Milton's most pathetic and human poem, "On his Deceased Wife," in which the once idealistic and ambitious young intellectual has finally and entirely submitted to the discipline of painful experience. It is chiefly from its purely private, particular details that the poem derives its initial power to move—above all in the sense of a thrice-lost wife, concealed from the start by blindness, for even in the dream of her return from death her face must be "veiled." Yet the poem does not ultimately leave one only with a memorable sense of the recurring shock of rediscovery with which a waking man must recognize the fact that he has become blind in the prime of life: "I wak'd, she fled, and day brought back my night." This sense of acute personal defeat is transcended in many ways. First by just that revelation of personal intimacy whose lack is the chilling factor in most of Milton's earlier English verse, and of which *Lycidas* is so bizarre an example. The lack of knowledge of his wife's face becomes a positive advantage because, unlike most people, Milton must respond to her purely in terms of personality, and cannot at all consider those more superficial genetic accidents or even merely cosmetic effects, which normally pass for beauty.

So that in a sense, if he is deprived of her thrice—in sight, by death, and in waking—he also recovers her thrice: first by discovering her real identity beyond the flesh he cannot see; secondly because his imagination is so deeply possessed of her existence that even death cannot prevent the persistence of her impression in his mind. The third factor is the most important and subtle: the poem clearly pivots around its eighth line (as do many sonnets): "I trust to have / Full sight of her in Heaven without restraint." One should note how deftly this powerful positive assertion is veiled by the lesser theme (but more intense shock) of one's rediscovered blindness so that ultimate confidence (of an irrational kind) coexists with immediate misery of great variety and sharpness. The survival of the positive in a harsh context is crucial: it is perhaps the only important psychological factor in the make-up of any human being. Its preeminence is the central tenet of Christianity and explains its extraordinary value to the suffering mind.

However, the poem does not casually assume the possibility of resurrection. And this is where Milton's neoclassicism dissolves into something more potent than Jonson's conscientious transposition and recreation of his models. The allusion to Hercules' rescue from death of Alcestis, the wife of his friend Admetus, is not a passing pedantic analogue but the kind of syncretism with which Christian humanists sought to confirm the

archetypal authority of biblical truth, as Auerbach
explained to us earlier. Thus the story of Deucalion
seemed to confirm Noah's historicity; and Socrates
prefigured the self-sacrifice of a later teacher. The choice
of Hercules was the more apt in that he is often taken
as an archetype of Christ (indeed Milton had used the
infant potency of the classical hero as an analogue to
Christ's in the Nativity Ode). In other words, in the
sonnet we are shown that it is universally accepted that
in some unintelligible way human heroism can rise
superior to the tragedies of life.

The choice of Admetus and Alcestis as the prototypes
is also a crucial one. How easily Milton could have
reverted to the flattering, sentimental, and pessimistic
allusion to Orpheus and Eurydice with which he had
ornamented *L'Allegro* and *Il Penseroso*. This would
have left Milton complacently admiring his own artistic
imagination while admitting its ultimate futility. The
triad of Hercules-Admetus-Alcestis is totally different
and far richer in human kindliness. As the husband,
Milton does *not* identify himself with the hero, the
rescuer (as he had flattered himself to be for his whole
country not so long ago). Rather he sees that the best
he can achieve is a passing dream of happiness leading
to a painful awakening, unless some unimaginable force
outside himself comes to his assistance. And the traditional role of Admetus carries only humiliating associations in its public aspect, since in Euripides, Admetus
is reduced to abject fear by the apprach of his death,
for which his wife courageously offers her own life as
substitute. Thus Milton is identified with the man who
survives but whose nerve and power is scarcely heroic.

However, if Admetus is totally unheroic in public, his character shows extraordinarily modern traits, in Euripides at least, which put him surprisingly in phase with Milton's mature views. Admetus is a failure as a king, everyone agrees about that. After his wife's death he loses all public authority just as the aging Milton did. But he never gives up in despair; and when his old friend Hercules drops in casually as was his wont, Admetus bravely tries to entertain his friend in the most hospitable way. The whole attitude is curiously like Milton's in writing the sonnets to his friends encouraging them to enjoy life and share his fellowship. It is in reward for this humble goodwill in the face of universal derision that Hercules undertakes to rescue Alcestis. Perhaps the avid study of Greek tragedy which occupied the blind Milton explains why this bizarre correlation should have caught his attention. In any event, the blind, ostracized, twice-widowed Milton finds his greatest worth in identifying with one of the most humiliated of Greek figures, because he sees in that frame of mind the likelihood of a greater salvation. The interesting thing is that having reached this good-natured pitch of humility Milton can ultimately become his own Hercules. And in *Samson* he seems to show that defeat is an almost inevitable prelude to ultimate, selfless heroism. Milton's last sonnet becomes an adequate measure of his previous political career, and a key to the purpose of his three major works with which he transcended his public defeat.

4: The Dream of Reason

W. H. Auden has written in *The Dyer's Hand* that "every work of a writer should be a first step, but this will be a false step unless, whether or not he realize it at the time, it is also a further step. When a writer is dead, one ought to be able to see that his various works, taken together, make one consistent *oeuvre*."[1] It is ironic that while this evolution has clearly appeared to us in Milton's minor verse, it largely fails to express itself in his prose. The conscious mind can obviously inhibit maturing if it is too devoted to system, logic, and all the absolute values which have been associated with the term "reason." From first to last Milton's prose remains largely of its time, and unlike his poetry it fails to grow consistently with the poet's own evolving experience. This is surely because the nominal goals which his academically trained reason set for him in his prose remained very much the same from 1644 when he published *Of Education* to the appearance of *A Ready and Easy Way to Establish a Free Commonwealth* in 1660. For there is still a certain naiveté evident even

[1] W. H. Auden, *The Dyer's Hand and Other Essays* (New York: Random House, 1962), p. 21.

in the title of this last proposal for a truly Platonic solution to England's political troubles.

The conventionality of Milton's ideas in his prose works is fully recognized by modern scholars, who share Arthur Barker's conviction that "Milton spoke in the language of his fellow pamphleteers. . . . The ideas he applied to the revolution bear a remarkable likeness to those employed by his fellows."[2] Moreover, such commentators have greatly intensified our sense of the conservative and secular foundations of the English reform movement as a whole, a movement concerned not so much with the advocacy of radical innovation, or any form of Calvinism, as with the rejection of Laudian "newfangledness." Don M. Wolfe has even argued that "Milton's rich contributions to the social idealism of the period, and his fruitful explorations of the springs of personality derived not the slightest inspiration from the dogma of Calvin."[3] If they do stem from any tradition, Wolfe feels these ideals mostly derive "from the broad humanism of the pagans." More recently Michael Fixler has confirmed this archaic strain in Milton's early ideology: "Evidently he thought the parallel objectives of spiritual perfection and social stability were to be achieved by restoration to primitive models rather than revolution and experimentation with new models."[4]

Merritt Hughes assents heartily to this recognition of the traditional character of Milton's political thought.

[2] Barker (see fn. 1, p. 215), p. xxi.

[3] Don M. Wolfe, *Milton in the Puritan Revolution* (New York: Thomas Nelson, 1941), p. 39.

[4] Michael Fixler, *Milton and the Kingdoms of God* (Evanston: Northwestern University Press, 1964), p. 94.

Writing of "Milton as Revolutionary" he wrily notes that "It is the uncompromisingly aristocratic cast of Milton's political thinking that is hard for the modern world to accept."[5] At best Hughes believes that Milton favored "the principle that Honor should go to men of talent rather than to men of family," and his various youthful Utopias certainly all do prefigure Michael Young's "Meritocracy." Hughes asserts that "in all of Milton's religious and political thinking . . . he was dominated by his confidence in the power of a half divine Right Reason to find out the Truth."[6] And he goes on to conclude that "his political thought in both his poetry and his prose was essentially Platonic. . . . Milton's prime concern was with the perfection of the state and the individual. That is why, in his first burst of revolutionary writing, in the anti-episcopalian tracts, he was more of a reformer than a revolutionist; and that is why, as he explored what Christian liberty meant to him in the divorce tracts, *Areopagitica*, the *Tenure*, and the later political pamphlets, he became more and more of a radical idealist."[7] Modern scholarship thus wholeheartedly confirms the Platonic aspects of Milton's ideology which I have isolated.

It is worth stressing that because of this ideology the weapons with which Milton fights in these prose works are often not even distinctively his own party's but rather those favored by his opponents also, as a result of a shared intellectual environment. Joseph Hall, Bishop of Exeter, set in motion one of the major controversial

[5] Merritt Y. Hughes, *Ten Perspectives on Milton* (New Haven: Yale University Press, 1965), p. 269 (hereafter cited as *Ten Perspectives*).

[6] *Ten Perspectives*, pp. 259-60.

[7] *Ten Perspectives*, pp. 274-75.

exchanges with his *Humble Remonstrance* in terms
anticipating those of *Areopagitica* when he asserted that
"we cannot prescribe to other men's thoughts; when
all is said, men will take liberty, (and who can hinder
it?) to abound in their own sense."[8] It is often, of course,
equally hard to differentiate Hall's tone from that of
his opponents, as when he indignantly observes that "if
any one resolve to continue unsatisfied, in spight of
reason, and all evidence of history, and will wilfully shut
his eies, with a purpose not to see the light, that man
is past my cure, and almost my pity."[9] On the other
hand, we find the same complacent sense of orthodoxy
among the supposed revolutionary opponents who challenge Hall's party in the no less traditional terms: "wee
finde that the late innovators which have so much
disturbed the peace and purity of our Church, did first
begin with the alteration of words. . . . The Church
of God hath alwayes been as diligent to resist novelities
of words, as her adversaries are busie to invent them."[10]
After all, Hall had begun by noting "the inconveniences
that do arise in Government, by admitting innovation."[11]
For supposed puritan reformers the Smectymnuus
group's sense of their own virtue is surprisingly complacent: "being conscious of our innocence and fidelity, we
could not but stand amazed and wonder to see ourselves
so unexpectedly and we hope undeservedly transformed
into men (or rather monsters of men) so transcen-

[8] Joseph Hall, *An Humble Remonstrance to the High Court of
Parliament* (London: M. F. for N. Butter 1640), p. 28.

[9] Hall, p. 21.

[10] Smectymnuus, *An Answer to a Book entitled, An Humble Remonstrance* (London: J. Rothwell, 1641), p. 92.

[11] Hall, p. 15.

dentally perfidious, and so supersuperlatively unfaithful and wicked."[12] One of their allies, Robert Greville, Lord Brooke, even went so far in upholding traditional order as to say that "I shall wholly agree, and joyne with them that endeavour with the first, to allay the very semblance and apparition (lesse than the least bubling up) of *Disorder.*"[13]

There is every indication that it is Brooke's urbane idealism and overt Platonism which provide crucial models for the ideology of the still naive Milton. In Brooke's mystically Platonic essay on *The Nature of Truth* we find, despite respectful notice of St. Paul, that Brooke rejects the Christian sense of human inadequacy almost entirely: "neither doe I at all abett that unhappy opinion of falling," holding rather "that the *Will* doth necessarily follow the *understanding*" for "what good we know, we are," and "Action dependeth wholly upon Knowledge."[14] In a famous phrase in his influential *Discourse Opening the Nature of that Episcopacie which is Exercised in England* Brooke speaks of "Right Reason; The Candle of God, which He hath lighted in Man, lest man groping in the Dark should stumble and fall." It is altogether to be expected that such confidence in human competence should lead to a complacent assumption of one's own rightness: "I desire to speak nothing but Truth. Yea, I should exceedingly rejoyce,

[12] Smectymnuus, *A Vindication of the Answer to the Humble Remonstrance* (London: John Rothwell, 1641), p. A4v.

[13] Robert Greville, Lord Brooke, *A Discourse Opening the Nature of that Episcopacie which is Exercised in England* (London: R. C. for S. Cartwright, 1641), p. 108 (hereafter cited as *Discourse*).

[14] Robert Greville, Lord Brooke, *The Nature of Truth* (London: R. Bishop for S. Cartwright, 1641; hereafter cited as *The Nature*), pp. 50, 58-59, 116.

if by the Spirit of Meeknesse, Men of that Learning, and abilities (which many of them are) might be reduced to that, which I from my soule conceive to bee truth, and am persuaded will be so acknowledged by Themselves, one day." Such naive confidence could only come from a conviction that "everything is either True or False" and that "God is the God of Order, and not of Confusion."[15] The same convictions govern even a Leveller like Gerrard Winstanley when he writes that "Man is called a reasonable creature, which is a name given to no other creature but men, because the Spirit of Reason appears acting in him, which if men did submit themselves unto, they would act righteously continually. . . . But the masculine powers of the poisoned flesh stand out against the King of Glory. . . . No man or woman, however, need be troubled at this for let every man cleanse himself of these wicked powers that rule him, and there speedily will be a harmony of love in the great creation."[16]

In such contexts we see that the earlier Milton is not distinctive but very much of his time, in the terms recently proposed by William Grace: "When he responds to the self-sufficiency of Hellenic tradition in regard to reason, Milton does look upon reason as a mistress absolute in herself," for "Milton takes a more optimistic view of the nature of man than is customary in Calvinistic theology." William Grace has no doubt of the ultimate derivation of Milton's views: "Milton's participation in public life follows an idealist pattern reminiscent of the philosopher-King in Plato's *Repub-*

---

[15] *Discourse*, pp. 29, 13, 29, 108.
[16] Quoted in Lewis H. Berens, *The Digger Movement* (London: Holland and Merlin, 1961), pp. 59-60.

lic." And in evaluating "the views of a Platonic Christian like Milton," Grace adds that they show "a certain nonhuman rather frigid aspect of Platonic Christianity."[17] Throughout the prose works we usually find Milton assuming the propriety of reliance upon a uniform human capacity for rational performance upon which he had himself reflected adversely much earlier in his presentation of the innocent children in *Comus*. And yet ten years after the masque, in *Of Education*, Milton was still capable of asserting that the aim of any education was to offset all those human inadequacies recognized in the doctrine of Original Sin: "The end then of learning is to repair the ruins of our first parents by regaining to know God aright, and out of that knowledge to love him, to imitate him, to be like him, as we may the nearest by possessing our souls of true virtue, which being united to the heavenly grace of faith makes up the highest perfection."[18] Faith and grace do finally receive a pious salute, but their function is more honorific than primary—after all, learning of itself can aim to repair the Fall, attain the knowledge of God, and even seek to gain equality with him, by the "possession of virtue." Inevitably faith here seems more like the final act of self-rectified will than the essential prerequisite for true understanding.

It is crucial to my purposes in this book that we see how inhibiting this positivist assumption of many seventeenth-century intellectuals is to Milton's career as a poet. If reason is sufficient for virtue, poetry is necessarily secondary and inferior. Milton's continued adherence

[17] William J. Grace, *Ideas in Milton* (Notre Dame: University of Notre Dame Press, 1968), pp. 49, 51, 54.

[18] Hughes, p. 631.

to his youthful idealism requires him over a long period
to reject the career of poet for that of pamphleteer, a
value judgment visibly reflected in his notorious comment on the relative immaturity of poetic values in his
program for students: "And now, lastly, will be the time
to read with them those organic arts which enable men
to discourse and write perspicuously, elegantly, and
according to the fitted style of lofty, mean, or lowly.
Logic, therefore, so much as is useful, is to be referred
to this due place with all her well-couched heads and
topics, until it be time to open her contracted palm into
a graceful and ornate rhetoric, taught out of the rule
of Plato. . . . To which poetry should be made subsequent, or indeed rather precedent, as being less subtle
and fine, but more simple, sensuous, and passionate."[19]
The almost conscious self-betrayal of his deeper instincts
in that last sentence appears in the uneasy and bizarre
shift from "subsequent" to its exact opposite: "precedent." Milton first unconsciously reveals that he sees
the affective role of poetry as climactic (that is, "subsequent") to rhetoric, even though his rationally conscious
mind at once strives to invalidate this Freudian slip by
making poetry only preliminary. Mere logic requires that
either "subsequent" or "precedent" be eliminated, but
instinct again intervenes and Milton fails fully to accomplish the choice against poetry, so his Platonic
values again reassert themselves, and more excessively,
causing him to expiate the fault by insulting his involuntarily cherished medium as "being less subtle and
fine." Poetry appears residually as Plato requires, merely
as a kind of attention-getting device appealing to the

[19] Hughes, pp. 636-37.

lesser, affective elements of personality: the view of Madison Avenue to this day.

The only worthy activity in such a value system aims at success in advocacy and teaching: in rating vocations Milton asserts that "laborious teaching is the most honorable prelaty that one minister can have above another."[20] Naturally Milton now devotes himself to the founding of a private Platonic academy in his own home to vindicate himself by educating society and particular individuals into that condition of virtue accessible to every reasonable man. This intellectual and social meliorism explains the form and tone of *Areopagitica*, the prose work which sums up the principles governing Milton's conscious mind during his career as pedagogue and propagandist. Milton framed the pamphlet as a speech because rhetoric, the highest and subtlest discipline, recognizes the sufficiency of reason to convince one's audience to act properly. Hence Milton's flowery and flattering claim that he is appealing to reason in his Parliamentary readers: "How much better I find ye esteem it to imitate the old and elegant humanity of Greece than the barbaric pride of a Hunnish and Norwegian stateliness. . . . But if from the industry of a life wholly dedicated to studious labours and those natural endowments haply not the worst for two and fifty degrees of northern latitude, so much must be derogated as to count me not equal to any of those who had this privilege [of addressing ancient parliaments, as a private person], I would obtain to be thought not so inferior as yourselves are superior to the most of them who received their counsel: and how far you excel them, be

---

[20] Hughes, p. 649.

assured, Lords and Commons, there can no greater testimony appear than when your prudent spirit acknowledges and obeys the voice of reason from what quarter soever it be heard speaking; and renders ye as willing to repeal any act of your own setting forth."[21]

As early as this point in the speech, contradictions which result in the failure of Milton's methods in his prose writings become apparent. Admirable as are the spirit and social awareness of *Areopagitica*, the speech presages its own ineffectiveness, for it is dependent on assumptions which are not only incompatible but mutually invalidating. An indication of this appears in the quoted passage: it is Milton's hope that mistakes already made by the governing body can be corrected because that body is held to be "willing to repeal any act of your own setting forth." This assumes that Parliament will agree that it is already demonstrably fallible; but if it is so deeply fallible, how can one accurately and reasonably predict its wise behavior on any future occasion either, or even at present? Indeed we can already detect that Milton has begun to admit to himself that his own mind was also limited by incapacity to live up to his own high expectations, and even by the incapacity to formulate these expectations satisfactorily.

For two years earlier, in the deeply self-revealing preface to the second book of *The Reason of Church Government*, Milton admits that Truth is a more elusive, painful, and unsatisfactory goal than his formal prose arguments usually allow: "How happy were it for this frail and, as it may be truly called, mortal life of

---

[21] Hughes, p. 719.

man, since all earthly things which have the name
of good and convenient in our daily use are withal so
cumbersome and full of trouble, if knowledge yet which
is the best and lightsomest possession of the mind, were,
as the common saying is, no burden, and that what is
wanted of being a load to any part of the body, it did
not with a heavy advantage overlay upon the spirit!
For not to speak of that knowledge that rests in the
contemplation of natural causes and dimensions , which
must needs be a lower wisdom, as the object is low,
certain it is that he who hath obtained in more than
the scantest measure to know anything distinctly of God
and of his true worship, and what is infallibly good and
happy in the state of man's life, what in itself evil and
miserable, though vulgarly not so esteemed—he that
hath obtained to know this, the only high valuable
wisdom indeed, remembering also that God even to a
strictness requires the improvement of these entrusted
gifts, cannot sustain a sorer burden of mind, and more
pressing, than any supportable toil or weight which the
body can labor under, how and in what manner he shall
dispose and employ those sums of knowledge and illumi-
nation which God hath sent him into this world. . . .
And although divine inspiration must certainly have
been sweet to those ancient prophets, yet the irkso-
meness of that truth which they brought was so un-
pleasant to them that everywhere they call it a burden."[22] Thus two years before *Areopagitica* Milton
already admits to a deep instinct against his planned
career as a propagandist and political activist; he claims
he is reluctant "to take up the trumpet and blow a

[22] Hughes, pp. 665-66.

dolorous or a jarring blast" and asks diffidently "For if I be, either by disposition or what other cause, too inquisitive or suspicious of myself and mine own doings, who can help it?"

However, Milton cannot yet assimilate these doubts of his chosen course to his sense of public obligation in the way he was finally able to do in showing Christ's repudiation of a career of activism in *Paradise Regained*. At this stage, even poetry must be true to the hortatory ideals set for it in *The Republic*, being "of power beside the office of a pulpit, to inbreed and cherish in a great people the seeds of virtue and public civility, to allay the perturbations of the mind and set the affections in right tune. . . . Teaching over the whole book of sanctity and virtue through all the instances of example, with such delight to those especially of soft and delicious temper who will not so much as look upon Truth herself, unless they see her elegantly dressed, that whereas the paths of honesty and good life appear now rugged and difficult, though they be indeed easy and pleasant, they would then appear to all men both easy and pleasant, though they were rugged and difficult indeed."[23]

The complete breakdown in consistency between these two passages from *The Reason of Church Government* illustrates the intrinsic antinomy of Milton's mental structures during the pamphleteering phase of his career. First, he regularly admits that he detests what he is doing, which is agonizingly painful and violates all his instincts; then in the very act of nostalgically (not to say extravagantly) praising the life he sadly rejects, he asserts that virtue is "easy and pleasant"

[23] Hughes, pp. 669-70.

and most readily advocated "to all men" by a person such as the poet he has just effectively refused to be. The same discontinuities reappear in *Areopagitica*. Ostensibly it is an appeal to the supposedly reasoned good sense of a Parliament which has nevertheless somehow mistakenly instituted a savage censorship. Yet the argument against censorship depends on the assertion that truth is difficult to identify, indeed likely at first to appear the height of error, for "if it come to prohibiting, there is not aught more likely to be prohibited than truth itself; whose first appearance to our eyes bleared and dimmed with prejudice and custom, is more unsightly and unplausible than many errors, even as the person is of many a great man slight and contemptible to see."[24] Milton provides the most telling personal illustration for his point, one that has become the classic case when he tells of how "I found and visited the famous Galileo, grown old, a prisoner to the Inquisition for thinking in astronomy otherwise than the Franciscan and Dominican licensers thought."[25]

The next stage of the situation is even more equivocal because even possession of the truth is no guarantee of virtue for "a man may be a heretic in the truth; and if he believe things only because his pastor says so, or the Assembly so determines, without knowing other reasons, though his belief be true, yet the very truth he holds becomes his heresy." Though I find this one of the most profound observations Milton ever wrote, it remains an argument terribly damaging to his case, for it admits that genuine accuracy of knowledge

[24] Hughes, p. 748.
[25] Hughes, p. 737-38.

may prove compatible with evil. Thus truth and wisdom appear very elusive, as is proved by Milton's own assertion "that those books, and those in great abundance which are likeliest to taint both life and doctrine. . . . are most and soonest catching to the learned, from whom the common people whatever is heretical or dissolute may quickly be conveyed. . . . Besides another inconvenience, if learned men be the first receivers out of books and dispreaders both of vice and error, how shall the licensers themselves be confided in, unless we can confer upon them, or they assume to themselves above all others in the land, the grace of infallibility and uncorruptedness."[26] From this sense of the overwhelming difficulty of recognizing and following truth, Milton proceeds in the very next paragraph to admonish his readers to "see the ingenuity of Truth, who, when she gets a free and willing hand, opens herself faster than the pace of method and discourse can overtake her."

No conceivable logic can rationalize this assertion, for the whole point of the treatise is that Parliament has already shown an insensibility to the truth which Milton has ascribed to those best qualified to judge it. Of course "a free and willing hand" for Truth was lacking, but when or how could this possibly be offered, since Milton asserts that Truth normally looks like egregious error, and all men anyway lack "the grace of infallibility and uncorruptedness"? While I agree with Milton that censorship is ridiculous because men are incapable of judging a truth in its formative stages, it does not follow from this that truth will necessarily prevail, but rather

[26] Hughes, p. 730.

the reverse. That truth must prevail is therefore not a valid argument for freedom of speech, and this is demonstrated by the total failure of the publication of *Areopagitica* to affect its Parliamentary audience. Not only the doctrine of Original Sin, but the mere logic of seventeenth-century history proves Milton wrong in his high estimate of "the natural wits of Britain" when he asks "what could a man require more from a nation so pliant and so prone to seek after knowledge? . . . A little generous prudence, a little forebearance of one another, and some grain of charity might win all these diligences to join and unite into one general and brotherly search after truth."[27]

One of the deepest ironies is that in the very pursuit of the freedom which he claims is inevitably productive of "the discovery that might yet be further made both in religious and civil wisdom," Milton firmly notes "I mean not tolerated popery and open superstition."[28] But if "Truth is strong, next to the Almighty"[29] why should superstition be dangerous and potentially stronger? If "God uses not to captivate under a perpetual childhood of prescription, but trusts [man] with the gift of reason to be his own chooser"[30] why preempt any choice, even Catholicism or witchcraft? And why should Milton himself as one of Cromwell's Censors of the Press many years later (1651-1652) be exempt from every error he ascribes to the best educated men, even in defense of the Commonwealth? The sad fact is that Milton cannot yet see the end of his own argument. Censorship

[27] Hughes, pp. 743-44.
[28] Hughes, pp. 720, 747.
[29] Hughes, p. 747.
[30] Hughes, p. 727.

is ridiculous because even the best of men may "let pass nothing but what is vulgarly received."[31] But the alternative is, by this very point, emphatically not "to be still searching out what we know not by what we know, still closing up truth to truth as we find it (for all her body is homogeneal and proportional)."[32] This is exactly the error Bacon is cited as censuring, for judging fresh ideas by "the language of the times."[33]

If all purely intellectual authority is abandoned (as I believe in all treatment of ideas and private morals it logically must be) the result will not be an immediate improvement in behavior, but apparent anarchy. This intellectual confusion will probably be no worse (and probably not much better) in negative cost than ideological repression; but at least such anarchy *may* evolve into something better (as an enforced mental order never can) along the lines of Blake's famous aphorism: "the road of excess leads to the palace of wisdom." It is to Milton's credit that he already senses this initially costly truth even as early as *Areopagitica*, when he observes: "were I the chooser, a dram of well-doing should be preferred before many times as much the forcible hindrance of evil-doing. For God sure esteems the growth and completing of one virtuous person more than the restraint of ten vicious."[34] But even the completion of that one virtuous person cannot presuppose at all times his spontaneous *avoidance* of evil and sure perception of truth. At the core of Milton's pamphlet lies his magnificent expansion of Paul's aphorism, which he

[31] Hughes, p. 736.
[32] Hughes, p. 742.
[33] Hughes, p. 736.
[34] Hughes, p. 733.

quotes: "Prove all things, hold fast that which is good" (I Thessalonians, 5, 21). Milton asserts we cannot tell good from bad until we have tried *both*: "As therefore the state of man now is, what wisdom can there be to choose, what continence to forbear without the knowledge of evil? He that can apprehend and consider vice with all her baits and seeming pleasures, and yet abstain, and yet distinguish, and yet prefer that which is truly better, he is the true warfaring Christian. I cannot praise a fugitive and cloistered virtue, unexercised and unbreathed, that never sallies out and sees her adversary, but slinks out of the race where that immortal garland is to be run for, not without dust and heat. Assuredly we bring not innocence into the world, we bring impurity much rather: that which purifies us is trial, and trial is by what is contrary. That virtue therefore which is but a youngling in the contemplation of evil, and knows not the utmost that vice promises to her followers, and rejects it, is but a blank virtue, not a pure."[35]

If this passage is the high point of the speech, as most readers assume, then it is clear that Milton's greatest interest lies far beyond the legal question of censorship, in the area of the learning process itself. And if wisdom in the Fallen World depends on the knowledge of evil won amidst "dust and heat" then the Platonic facility in rational analysis deserves the censure Milton soon after gives it when he observes that: "Plato, a man of high authority indeed, but least of all for his commonwealth, in the book of his *Laws*, which no city ever yet received, fed his fancy with making many edicts to his airy burgomasters, which they who otherwise admire

[35] Hughes, p. 728.

him, wish had been rather buried and excused in the
genial cups of an Academic night-sitting."[36] Yet this
facility of analysis is precisely what renders the far later
pamphlet, *A Ready and Easy Way*, as nugatory as the
Laws, and scarcely less repressive and embittered. One
is left wondering how a Milton already aware of the
need to temper the heat of virtue to a cooler wisdom
by experience of an evil world could ever hope to achieve
any real change in his contemporaries by merely rational
arguments. He seems himself "but a youngling in the
contemplation of evil" when he trusts in "the natural
wits of Britain," a nation he describes as "so pliant and
so prone to seek after knowledge."[37]

The inadequacy of the naive optimism of these concluding phrases of *Areopagitica* is not only stressed by
our recollection of the simplicities of the inept brothers
in *Comus*; we can also see how Milton's hindsight
undercuts it retrospectively in his last major poems.
Take this hearty image: "Methinks I see in my mind
a noble and puissant nation rousing herself like a strong
man after sleep, and shaking her invincible locks"[38]—and
put it next to *Samson Agonistes*. The ominous overtones
of the sentence from *Areopagitica* are disturbing, once
the most significant Bibilical context is recognized: the
strong man, Samson, did *not* rise from sleep stronger
on the occasion we first recall, but weaker—and the
confusion of genders in the sentence oddly enough
reminds us that it *is* a female who shakes those "invincible locks": Dalila. The inadequacy of Milton's youthful

[36] Hughes, p. 731.
[37] Hughes, p. 743.
[38] Hughes, p. 745.

thought produces a hopelessly garbled set of associations in his prose of which he would never be guilty in his maturity, or in his best verse.

This kind of incompetence also extends much deeper, to the very arguments themselves. If "that which purifies us is trial, and trial is by what is contrary," then the following statement is invalid: "Ye cannot make us now less capable, less knowing, less eagerly pursuing of the truth, unless ye first make yourselves, that made us so, less the lovers, less the founders of our true liberty. We can grow ignorant again, brutish, formal, and slavish as ye found us; but you then must first become that which ye cannot be, oppressive, arbitrary, and tyrannous, as they were from whom ye have freed us. That our hearts are now more capacious, our thoughts more erected to the search and expectation of greatest and exactest things, is the issue of your own virtue propagated in us."[39] Yet what generated this new energy was the reformers' increasing awareness of the evils of the Stuart establishment and not the virtues of Members of Parliament, or of the Presbyterians, or of the English people, who progressively from this period earn from Milton clearer recognition, as "apostate scarecrows" and "disturbers of the civil affairs" anxious to "assist the clamor and malicious drifts of men whom they themselves have judged to be the worst of men, the obdurate enemies of God," and thereby showing they actually seek "the worthless approbation of an inconstant, irrational, and image-doting rabble."[40]

---

[39] Hughes, p. 745-46.
[40] Hughes, pp. 752, 772, 815.

Milton's political pamphlets, and above all the best
of them, *Areopagitica*, thus contain their own disproof
of the value of rational reform. They argue rationally
over issues with obtuse authorities, whose mere bigoted
existence refutes the possibility of reasoned progress.
And as the pamphlets continue to flow from Milton's
pen this irreducible schism of idealistic theory and
historical fact causes increasingly bitter symptoms of
tension to appear in the author's own mind. On the
one hand Milton's sense of his own rationality and
rectitude drives him to harsher and harsher attacks on
almost all his contemporaries: "If men within themselves would be governed by reason and not generally
give up their understanding to a double tyranny of
custom from without and blind affections within; they
would discern better what it is to favor and uphold the
tyrant of a nation. But being slaves within doors, no
wonder that they strive so much to have the public
state conformably governed to the inward vicious rule
by which they govern themselves. For, indeed, none can
love freedom heartily but good men."[41] Yet, if it turns
out that there are few if any good men, this inevitably
becomes an argument for dictatorship and tyranny as
extreme as that adopted by the ruined Stuart establishment. In his last pamphlet, despite his affectation of
libertarianism, Milton sounds in tone more like Strafford, or Laud, or even Hobbes than like Marvell and
his Whig successors in his view of the English people.
He describes them as a people whose "greatest part have
both in reason and the trial of just battle lost the right
of their election what the government shall be." And

[41] Hughes, p. 750.

he continues, "Of them who have not lost that right, whether they for kingship be the greatest number, who can certainly determine? Suppose they be, yet of freedom they partake all alike, one main end of government; which if the greater part value not, but will degenerately forego, is it just or reasonable that most voices against the main end of government should enslave the less number that would be free? More just it is, doubtless, if it come to force that a less number compel a greater ... be the voices never so numerous that oppose it."[42]

And as he comes to recognize the folly and irrationality of the whole of the rest of humankind, far from seeing that his own ostensibly rational and melioristic views are intensifying the very misanthropy which discredits these ideas, Milton becomes ever more neurotically rigid in his affirmation of his own rightness in all his values, choice, and actions. He advises his critics to "consider that my situation, such as it is, is neither an object of my shame or my regret, that my resolutions are too firm to be shaken, that I am not depressed by any sense of divine displeasure; that on the other hand, in the most momentous periods, I have had full experience of the divine favor and protection; and that, in the solace and the strength which have been infused into me from above, I have been enabled to do the will of God: that I may oftener think on what he has bestowed than on what he has withheld; that in short, I am unwilling to exchange my consciousness of rectitude with that of any other person; and that I feel the recollection a treasured store of tranquility and delight."[43] One is reminded of Oedipus or Pentheus, for

[42] Hughes, p. 895.
[43] Hughes, p. 826.

beneath all its aggressiveness the assertion has an una-
vowed nervous tension. It is not accidental that (like
the Lady's in *Comus*) the neurotic fixity of this view,
"that my resolutions are too firm to be shaken," is echoed
in a trait ascribed to Satan who also asserts that he
is "One who brings / A mind not to be chang'd by Place
or Time" (I. 252-53). It is shortly after the passage just
quoted from the *Defense* that Milton recites his idealized
self-portrait, in which all the limitations of his career
are suppressed, and glories in his heroic defiance of the
Pope "in the very metropolis of popery"—[44] a feat
reflecting at least as much credit on the forbearance
of the Roman Catholics as on the confidence of their
Puritan visitor.

The tone of Milton to his opponents from this point
on approximates that which Swift ascribed to the misanthropic Gulliver after his return from his trip to the
country of the inhumanly rational horses. Milton ad-
monishes them: "You, therefore, who wish to remain
free, either instantly be wise or, as soon as possible, cease
to be fools. If you think slavery an intolerable evil, learn
obedience to reason and the government of yourselves,
and finally bid adieu to your dissentions, your jealousies,
your superstitions, your outrages, your rapine, and your
lusts. Unless you will spare no pains to affect this, you
must be judged unfit, both by God and mankind to be
entrusted with the possession of liberty and the admin-
istration of the government, but will rather, like a nation
in a state of pupilage, want some active and courageous
guardian to undertake the management of your affairs."[45]

[44] Hughes, p. 829.
[45] Hughes, pp. 837-38.

The cult of reason thus leads Milton directly to the threat of a tyranny comparable to that which Strafford's "thorough" program proposed to establish for the Stuarts. But above all we must note the crassness of Milton's naive imperatives: "either instantly be wise or cease to be fools," so sardonically caricatured by Swift in Gulliver's Prefatory Letter to his Cousin Sympson: "instead of seeing a full stop put to all Abuses and Corruptions, at least in this little Island, as I had reason to expect: Behold, after above six Months warning, I cannot learn that my book hath produced one single Effect according to mine Intentions: I desired you would let me know by Letter, when Party and Faction were extinguished; Judges learned and upright; Pleaders honest and modest, with some Tincture of Common Sense; . . . Wit, Merit and Learning rewarded. . . . These, and a Thousand other Reformations, I firmly counted upon by your Encouragement; as indeed they were plainly deducible from the Precepts delivered in my Book. And, it must be owned that seven Months were a sufficient Time to correct every Vice and Folly."[46] The fictional Gulliver at least allowed seven months for reform, presumably because Swift felt anything hastier would seem too grotesque for his readers; but the historical Milton requires *his* readers to "instantly be wise."

In the late fifties Milton thus begins to sound like a misanthropic extremist, of whom Shakespeare's Coriolanus is another prototype:

You common cry of curs, whose breath I hate
As reek o' th' rotten fens, whose loves I prize

[46] Jonathan Swift, *Gulliver's Travels etc.* (New York: Random House, 1949), p. 6.

As the dead carcasses of unburied men
That do corrupt my air, I banish you!

(III.iii.121-24)

Ultimately the simpleminded polarization of values even becomes reminiscent of *Timon of Athens* for, on the one hand, in terms of excellence: "the way propounded is plain, easy and open before us, without intricacies,"[47] yet, on the other, the bestial English persist in rejecting it and also Milton's plea, "though they seem now choosing them a captain back for Egypt, to bethink themselves a little and consider whither they are rushing; to exhort this torrent also of the people not to be so impetuous, but to keep their due channel; and at length recovering and uniting their better resolutions, now that they see already how open and unbounded the insolence and rage is of our common enemies, to stay these ruinous proceedings, justly and timely fearing to what a precipice of destruction the deluge of this epidemic madness would hurry us, through the general defection of a misguided and abused multitude."[48]

This sentence marks the climactic point of Milton's ambivalence, for the very people he exhorts to accept his republican solution are also the leaders of the insane mob whom he compares to the herd of Gadarene Swine hurling themselves off the heights of liberty to drown themselves in a restored monarchism. It is scarcely surprising that, as Parker notes, within a few days of the publication of the pamphlet its printer had to flee since "an order for his arrest was issued by the Council

[47] Hughes, p. 892.
[48] Hughes, p. 899.

of State."[49] So hostile was the general reception of the essay that it was destroyed almost completely, and only three known copies survive: the rational reformer found that he "stood almost alone."[50] From the dream of utopian reason Milton now woke to the nightmare of political reality: universally execrated, blind, and in hiding, he saw everything he had argued for derided and repudiated. Ironically, only the completeness of his ruin probably saved him from the punishments inflicted on the few feeble remnants of his party; at the age of fifty-one he obviously seemed, as Parker observes, doomed to a vestigial career as a "nightmarish monster" living "in perpetual terror of being assassinated."[51] The idealistic reformer had failed irrecoverably. Milton's career as a Christian revolutionary was about to begin.

[49] William R. Parker, *Milton: A Biography* (Oxford: Clarendon Press, 1968), I, 556.

[50] Parker, I, 557.

[51] Parker, I, 576-77.

5: *Paradise Lost:*
The Uses of Adversity

John Keats' artless aspiration that his career might be crowned by the writing of "a few great plays" has been greeted with a certain wryness even by sympathetic modern critics. No such censure attends the scarcely more reasonable expectations of the nineteen-year-old John Milton in advising the English language:

Yet I had rather, if I were to choose,
Thy service in some graver subject use,
Such as may make thee search thy coffers round,
Before thou clothe my fancy in fit sound:
Such where the deep transported mind may soar
Above the wheeling poles, and at Heav'n's door
Look in, and see each blissful Deity . . .
Then sing of secret things that came to pass
When Beldam Nature in her cradle was;
And last of Kings and Queens and Heroes old,
Such as the wise Demodocus once told
In solemn Songs at King Alcinous' feast,
While sad Ulysses' soul and all the rest
Are held with his melodious harmony.

Other youthful glimpses of epic achievement abound in this period of Milton's career, indicating his hope to write a kind of British *Æneid* based on King Arthur. As late as 1642 he is still preoccupied enough with the project to include in the Preface to the Second Book of *The Reason of Church Government* an "account of what the mind at home in the spacious circuits of her musing hath liberty to propose herself, though of highest hope and hardest attempting; whether that epic form whereof the two poems of Homer and those other two of Virgil and Tasso are a diffuse, and the book of Job a brief model: or whether the rules of Aristotle herein are strictly to be kept, or nature to be followed, which in them that know art and use judgment, is no transgression but an enriching of art: and lastly, what king or knight before the conquest might be chosen in whom to lay the pattern of a Christian hero."[1]

What Milton here avoids considering (just as Keats did later) is that art is like virtue in not being simply a matter of form or the product of volition alone. One might confidently predict that if Milton's project had been achieved before the Commonwealth it would have risked the unevenness of *Comus* or *The Faerie Queene*. The first step toward deeper creativity necessarily lay in the failure of Milton's shallow confidence both in his own capacities and in the formal approaches to the genre which he favored. Paradoxically, the realization of his epic goal was impossible as long as he confidently expected it; and rather than lamenting Milton's deflection into pamphleteering, we should therefore see that only its cataclysmic failure could have served as a prelude for a truly epic vision, to which mere youthful ambition cannot aspire without risk of ridicule. Despite Aristotle's preference for tragedy, with its greater immediacy and accessibility, epic has remained the senior

[1] Hughes, pp. 668-69.

literary form for a variety of reasons, some of which
Milton could only partly understand in his more confident moods before the Restoration.

He was, of course, right to assume that the supreme
role of epic lies in its capacity to focus a society's
self-awareness in a more comprehensive way than is
possible in a single drama, or even in a novel on any
scale less than *War and Peace*. For the Greeks, Homer
defined the genesis and values of their culture, much
as the Pentateuch did for the Hebrews; but neither of
these sources could be summed up as the confident
affirmation of national identity Milton is still guilty of
in the peroration of *Areopagitica* in 1643, where he
praises England as "this nation chosen before any
other." Mere positive illustration of virtue is as alien
to the epic as it is to tragedy: rather the great primary
epics deal with their cultures at some primitive moment
of crisis which they can barely survive, or which even
seems to defeat them through the kind of challenge
which Toynbee defines as the source of all cultural
evolution. Thus the Hellenes of the *Iliad* are by no
means idealized or confident of success, and their victory
seems terribly precarious and marginal; the end of
Beowulf comes with the death of its protagonist and
the sense of the impending extinction of his people; *The
Song of Roland* leaves one deeply uneasy about the
viability and plausibility of the so-called "Christian
chivalry" which it is supposed to glorify.

In this sense, the failure of the Puritan Commonwealth and the savage revaluation of his native land
which it forced upon Milton were necessary prerequisites
for true epic awareness. The response which such defeats

evoke from him as early as *The Tenure of Kings and Magistrates* serves as an intensely felt equivalent to the epic failures of Achilles, Beowulf, or Roland: " 'Tis true that most men are apt enough to civil wars and commotions as a novelty, and for a flash hot and active; but through sloth or inconstancy and weakness of spirit, either fainting ere their own pretenses, though never so just, be half attained, or through an inbred falsehood and wickedness, betray ofttimes to destruction with themselves, men of noblest temper joined with them for causes whereof they in their rash undertakings were not capable."[2] This is the ominous note of true epic, but at the time of writing the pamphlet Milton had obviously not come to accept this view as inevitable, and it is striking to see how now and later in his career he instinctively tends toward writing in a lesser (but still epic) mode than this primary form: the discursive epic associated with Boeotia through Hesiod's *Theogony* and his *Works and Days*.

At first sight this clumsy kind of metrical encyclopedia may seem to have little stature in comparison with the drastic splendors of the primary epic, but this "secondary" kind of epic is surprisingly vital and influential, particularly if we recognize that its flexible patterns readily assimilate such widely ranging works as Lucretius' *De Rerum Naturae*, Ovid's *Fasti* and *Metamorphoses*, Virgil's *Georgics*, Langland's *Piers Ploughman*, Du Bartas' *Holy Weeks*, and even such contemporary, apparent monstrosities as Pound's *Cantos*. The literary unfashionableness of many of these works often correlates directly with their popular appeal and impact:

[2] Hughes, p. 751.

unlike the works of most of his Renaissance contemporaries, Thomas Tusser's *Points of Husbandry* has hardly ever been out of print. The didactic force of such discursive works corresponds to the attitudes which we find in Milton's pamphleteering period and in *Areopagitica* above all: "What could a man require more from a nation so pliant and so prone to seek after knowledge? What wants there to such a towardly and pregnant soul but wise and faithful laborers to make a knowing people, a nation of prophets, of sages, and of worthies."[3] Clearly the second, encyclopedic form of epic also closely corresponds to the didactic type of poetry which Plato would allow into his ideal Republic. Yet the mode shares the limitations of the first kind of epic which make it less pleasing and accessible than other, more sophisticated genres. As the result of an accumulative growth of traditional materials transcending individual authorship, the effect of both these kinds of epics often seems (wrongly and superficially) to be jerky and inconsistent. The truths of the collective unconscious have a lack of smoothness and sentimental focus which has been successfully offset by the third great epic mode: the tale of Everyman. Here, instead of the complex interaction of whole societies and continents in historically documented works like the *Iliad*, we characteristically find the picturesque tracing out of one representative man's life, whether it be that of Ulysses, Gilgamesh, or even Dante himself. This more personal third mode has proved the most fertile of the three types of epic described, and without its essential focus on the fate of

[3] Hughes, p. 743.

an individual with whom we empathize, the epic genre would have had little modern chance of survival.

Indeed we might conclude our definition of epic modes by creating a fourth epic form: a syncretic epic aesthetically fusing all three of the other types under the pressure of the personal excitement and interest generated by audience involvement with a single figure of the third mode. The *Æneid* is a precedent for the quaternary epic by its blend of mass cultural conflicts, historical and geographical comprehensiveness, and focus on the romantic career of Æneas. However, the poem's ultimate emotional focus has generally been felt not to be Æneas but Virgil's own private feelings; and it is Dante's distinction to bring out this veiled but crucial authorial interest of the *Æneid* in his own definitive version of the quaternary epic, *The Divine Comedy*. In making the historical author himself the Everyman figure, Dante achieved a decisive modernization of the genre by enormously enriching its subjectivity in ways which opened it up to developments as varied as *Paradise Lost, The Prelude,* and even perhaps *A la Recherche du Temps Perdu.*

For if we trace Milton's career, we shall see how he is unwillingly and unwittingly forced step by step to accommodate himself and his experience to the diverse demands of the epic traditions described above. His confrontation with the failure of the English to realize their full potentialities for reformation drives him beyond an interest in bellicose heroism to inquire what may be the didactic resources to foster virtuous action offered by Western culture, and to focus these dramatically on the archetypal figures of Adam and Eve as they

appear to an overtly contemporary observer, who is
deliberately equated with the historical narrator himself.
Each epic mode is given its full weight in this masterly
synthesis: the traditional violence and precarious values
of the primary epic reappear in Satan and the Battle
in Heaven; the didactic exposition of an encyclopedic
world-view in the long speeches of Raphael and Michael;
the sentimental human focus in the marriage of Adam
and Eve; and the contemporary need for personal immediacy and point of view in the crucial authorial intru-
sions, above all at the start of Books I, III, VII, and
IX.[4] But the center of this pattern lies outside any single
element of it. Faced with the seeming wreck of his career
and the disaster of the Restoration, Milton set himself
a truly epic goal: not of flattering his compatriots nor
ultimately even of educating them into their ideal state
of virtue, but of assimilating the apparently continuous
failure of occidental culture to do any better than its
recent English fragment. This goal of reconciliation to
human failure makes *Paradise Lost* the first and greatest epic of the pessimistic modern European consciousness, just as *The Divine Comedy* is the only true
epic of medieval Christendom, with its more confident
expectations: the title of Milton's *Paradise Lost* con-
trasts ominously with Dante's "comic" vision of Paradise
Won.

Dante's poem is consciously an account of the human
potentiality for success. Even the failures of its first
phases are seen to be offset by the progressive pattern

[4] A masterly discussion of the authorial role appears in W. G. Riggs,
The Christian Poet in "Paradise Lost" (Berkeley: University of California Press, 1972).

of amelioration which is the underlying structure of the poem, one which according to Nygren quite clearly illustrates a Platonic hierarchy of self-improvement depending on ratiocination and didacticism rather than a spontaneous act of grace transcending logic. The human Christ never directly appears in Dante's epic, for his reversal of the Platonic ascent is reflected only in the supercilious and limited condescension of a Beatrice, who herself scarcely deigns to pass the borders of Paradise to help in the rescue of her lover. As Nygren has demonstrated in *Agape and Eros*, the Thomist structure of *The Divine Comedy* owes all too much to pagan trust in Reason, and this carries the penalty of accepting the aristocratic hierarchy for which Auerbach implicitly indicts classical culture in the early chapters of *Mimesis*. Dante's sense of human capacity in his poem corresponds closely with the assumptions of Milton's prose, and it leads him as often to that vitriolic and merciless censure of human failure which has unfortunately but understandably alienated nonacademic readers from both men.

But if Dante outlines the techniques for success in a kind of cosmic social climbing, Milton's epic by contrast is essentially the Anatomy of Failure. Dante moves human awareness relentlessly toward the inhumanely transcendent triangle which crowns his cosmic pyramid; but Milton crushes all human knowledge and experience through the humble and accessible locus of failure provided by Adam's Original Sin. Dante leaves the Fallen World behind; Milton insists that we endure it, at most following Dante only as far as the moment when he struggles out of the hysteria of Hell into the more hopeful mental climate of Purgatory. Milton's epic addresses itself to the great question which has haunted, indeed blasted, modern consciousness: what can be made of a world full of evil and suffering? His epic is a monumental accumulation of every resource bearing on the question of how wrong choices are made, and on what our response to them should be once they have been accomplished.

Milton's methods are far less artificial than is usually imagined. He is concerned first with schematic diagnosis: to sketch in the broad outlines of factors contributing to wrong choices and consequent failures. The first half of *Paradise Lost* is essentially a conceptualization of the psychology of failure, comparable in technique to the kind of theoretical schema we would expect in the abstract outlining of a psychosis or neurosis—say the generalized characteristics of schizophrenia, manic-depression, or the Oedipus complex. We should recognize that in angelology Milton had a system just as valid for the description of abstract mental entities, forces, and symptoms as any modern psychiatry. Indeed a case could be made for the superior flexibility and comprehensiveness of the traditional metaphysics and symbolism of Christianity to the crude and rigid categories of current psychology. By the use of concrete data from history, and by including his own friends and enemies, Dante had enormously enriched the medieval terminology of psychological analysis so that it scarcely resembled the crudely formal allegory of the battle between the Virtues and Vices we find in the fourth-century *Psychomachia* of Prudentius. But Dante intended his figures (including himself) to be at best "concrete uni-

versals" or "objective correlatives" for conceptual patterns, and one of the classic failings of modern readers
is to insist that Dante's characters are not abstractions
from Dante's experience, though reflecting back on it,
but are the real people themselves. Unfortunately, most
moderns have lost the capacity to read anything in
another sense than the literal, so that when the narrator
of *The Divine Comedy* treats a figure in Hell harshly,
we tend not to realize that this "means" that we should
treat that kind of mental aberration severely when we
see it in ourselves, but to feel as if Dante were literally
being fierce to an old acquaintance when he meets him
in some actual street.

The vividness of Dante's poetic recapture of his past
life makes this error understandable (and he probably
was pretty severe in real life anyway); but the same
mistake made by Satanists in reading *Paradise Lost*
is far less pardonable. The assumption that one would
naturally and instinctively ally oneself emotionally with
Satan in the first half of *Paradise Lost* suggests such
ethical ineptitude as to prove that one is not of the
"fit audience . . . though few" to whom Milton frankly
limited himself. Empathy with Satan is roughly equivalent to loving tuberculosis, or at least schizophrenia.
One can hardly love a disease without willful perversity,
even if it does have romantic associations (and Alethea
Hayter's *Opium and the Romantic Imagination* has
shown that great art never results directly from afflic-
tion, but rather from the resistance to it—even in the
Romantic Age). The essential point about Satan is that
he is consistently an angelic (that is, intellectual) principle, not a person. He has no more of a complete and

historical identity than does Adler's idea of the Inferior-
ity Complex, or Freud's Super-Ego. Compared with
Adam and Eve, Satan is only a single element of human
consciousness. What we have in the first half of the
epic is thus a highly abstract pathology of mental
disease, or at least of the neurotic factors leading to
false choices. It is possible to show that Milton was aware
of what he was doing because of his handling of the
various associated mental traits grouped round the
Satan principle in the guise of diabolic cohorts. These
plausibly reappear in the second half of the poem as
psychological traits, or realistic thought patterns, enter-
ing the minds of Adam and Eve, but never to the
exclusion of all else in the way of personality as they
do in their initial roles as Moloch, Belial, or Satan
himself.

If we review the sweep of the first six books of *Paradise
Lost* from this perspective, almost all the details become
startlingly, not to say narrowly, functional, and most
of the supposed "problems" disappear. Milton starts
with the basic subject: the condition of the aspiring mind
insofar as it is forcibly concerned with its own crushing
failure. This condition would be analogous to a develop-
ing awareness in Milton's own mind which probably
stretched over many years, but which surely reached
a climax during 1661 after his ambitious hopes of creating a new order of state for England had failed as grossly
as Satan's. At such a moment, the ambitious mind often
suffers an almost complete mental and physical black-
out, and the imagery of the epic's first book correctly
accumulates impressions appropriate to the dictionary
definition of advanced catatonia: "characterized by

stupor, muscular-rigidity, and occasional mental agitation." This state results classically from the unendurable shattering of a pure egotism which is solipsistically unwilling to tolerate the idea of its own lack of self-sufficiency—a resistance epitomized by rebellion against the archetypal Father-Image. Such a mind repudiates the primacy of any other interests but its own, as illustrated in the rejection of the claim to Satan's respect made by the Son. Satan revolts from anything incompatible with his own absolute autonomy: a response which is the mark of the primal selfishness of infancy and which human maturity necessarily tempers to reasonable demands for social acceptance. The relationship between the Father, his Son, and Satan in the first books of *Paradise Lost* is thus a universal pattern of social psychology having nothing of quaint and moribund myth about it.

What is memorable is how Milton has brought the pattern into almost hallucinatory visibility by encrusting it with myriad glittering allusions to every aspect of this archetypal relationship known to Western man. God the Father is not only the Christian figure, but the Jewish Jehovah, and the Primum Mobile of neo-Aristotelian metaphysics. As a mere part of Creation, Satan is shown willfully to deny his secondary nature to such ultimate referents, in effect denying the universal reality-principle itself. Rather than admit his own secondary status, he characteristically insists that the whole cosmos is not what it has obviously seemed to be to any perceptive culture. He locks himself up in his own partial and darkened awareness, and thereby locks the whole universe out except insofar as it can be forced to fragment itself into a disorder assimilable to his own rigid idea: hence the alliances with Chaos, Sin, and Death. Only madness or disintegration of what exists objectively outside itself will allow this kind of absolute egotism to maintain its own morbid introversion.

There is also great psychological acuteness in Milton's identification of the principle invested in the Son whom Satan refuses to serve. What egotism (Satan) here rejects is the principle of love and creativity epitomized in the account of the Creation, a principle which is an intrinsic part of God the Father insofar as he makes *anything* beyond himself and concerns himself with it—that is, turns his attention away from contemplating himself exclusively. So the opening schema of *Paradise Lost* displays a perfectly expressed theological pattern. The primal act of creation involves a subordination of even the ultimate private self to something other (making it technically inferior or dependent). Satan is thus in a sense the principle of self-esteem of the Platonic Ideal contemplating itself to the exclusion of all else, and the love of the secondary and lesser, epitomized by the nature of the Son, necessarily itself seems "secondary" to this primal complacency, and incompatible with it. The quarrel between Satan and the Son has thus ultimately nothing personal in it. It depends on a seeming metaphysical incompatibility betweeen the idea of the ultimately perfect and the idea of its creation, and its consequent recognition, of that which is secondary, an incompatibility for which few nominalistic metaphysical systems in the Platonic tradition (including Dante's Thomism) have been able to account.

However, the first six books of *Paradise Lost* do not depend solely on a metaphysical pattern skillfully swathed in allegories derived from what now resemble psychiatric observations. Milton cleverly exploits the political dimensions of the secular morality play to allow for a sequential investigation of the theme simultaneously in both a psychological and a political frame of reference. The moods associated with pathological egotism are objectified in a debate in which the rationalizations of the diseased mind are equated with the public personae of political life. In Moloch we see the mood of suicidal despair of the last days of the Third Reich, when self-destruction by fatal prolongation of a lost fight was preferred to acceptance of the fact of defeat with the hope of salvaging something from the ruin. The trial of Charles Manson's tribe threw up similar manifestations of neurotic and self-destructive willfulness in the accused.

Other alternatives to creative acceptance of failure include Belial's sensual apathy, or Mammon's refuge from admission of defeat in a distracting but pointless aesthetic activity. But the most sinister response of all remains Satan's own: the decision that everything which is incompatible with egotistical satisfaction must be destroyed as far as possible. Thus ideally all creation must be returned to primal chaos or nonexistence. Even this extravagant response has its political equivalent, as we see in the traditional holocaust which many an absolutist demands of his subjects on the accomplishment of his own death: no one personally known to him shall have the satisfaction of surviving his master's defeat. The scorched-earth policy and wanton destructiveness of many unsuccessful revolutionary movements show similar nihilistic tendencies. Ironically the metaphysical dimension is fully consonant with this pattern: if what is created is destroyed, then the Creator's primal egotism is necessarily fully reconstituted, for he has once more nothing to contemplate but himself.

We must not neglect the private dimension to this pattern, however. Milton's role in the epic is to give the local, contemporary application to his theme, showing how it applies to any modern individual like ourselves. Like Satan, Milton had expected to enforce the superiority of his own political vision upon the whole English nation, but also like Satan had found himself cast down into hellish darkness, in despair of all future success. His refuge similarly lies in finding a way to preserve his fading subjective vision. In a sense, completing a great epic after practical failure could be an aesthetic evasion of painful realities comparable to the construction of Pandemonium to conceal one's hellish situation, or to attempting to capture a new and lesser world of private people's minds, having failed either to scale the heights of Paradise or "build a new Jerusalem in England's green and pleasant land."

To claim solipsistically that one speaks with the authority of God is a natural and ominous compensation for a failing politician. How seriously Milton takes this issue appears in his careful analysis of the way in which, like Satan, he himself escapes from passive despair. In each of the authorial speeches beginning Books III and VII Milton affirms that what he is doing is not the result of any authority or resource vested in his own talents and insight. He humbly salutes the light of heaven as

if he had less ambitiously duplicated Satan's journey
himself, having:

> Escap't the *Stygian* Pool, though long detain'd
> In that obscure sojourn, while in my flight
> Through utter and through middle darkness borne
> With other notes than to th' *Orphean* Lyre
> I sung of *Chaos* and *Eternal Night*,
> Taught by the heav'nly Muse to venture down
> The dark descent, and up to reascend,
> Though hard and rare.
>
> (III, 14-21)

The stress on the fact that he writes "umpremeditated
verse," at the start of Book IX, is equally designed to
reject any aspiration to conscious achievement, which,
being willed, would justify egotistical pride of a Satanic
kind. Milton rejects intellectual ambition and accepts
the Christian doctrine of a divinity who is emotionally
committed to the well being and direct inspiration of
what are secondary, dependent, and inferior: his own
creations.

Milton thus manages to cover the whole range of
possible allusion in the first six books of his epic: he
assimilates pagan philosophy, classical and biblical history, and his own seventeenth-century experience. Yet
the postulated modesty of his role forbids that Milton
become the formal hero of his own epic as Dante's more
confident world view had allowed him to be. Milton uses
as his human focus the archetypal figures of Adam and
Eve, who alone in the work show in full detail the
psychological progressions of complete human personalities; even the powers of the Trinity in the poem are

in some senses only partial, if positive, abstractions of human personalities matching the diabolic neuroses seen in Satan and his cohorts. The first state of innocence in Eden is not simply a clever literary trick showing Milton's skill at redeploying the literary resources of the pagan myth of the Age of Gold to enrich the economical biblical story. Milton wants above all to conjure up the sense of naive life shared equally by the classical and biblical stories and by every immature human being, including Milton himself—his own innocent *L'Allegro* contributes much to the texture of this phase of the poem. The problem which all these allusions postulate is the same: granted the youthful positiveness and innocence of the whole human race, or of individual, primitive societies, or of the single person—how does this happy state evolve with such inevitability to total disaster? Why does the Age of Gold finally sink to that of Iron?—and Adam make the mistake which forever exiles him from Eden?—above all why does the inexperienced child become the corrupt adult?

Is it because the universe is so consistently evil that mankind cannot but fail? This is the Satanic view: "I am not to blame." But the epic labors long to prove that this excuse will not serve Adam and Eve; they reflect the best of human experience by receiving every kind of advice, warning, aid, and protection and yet still plausibly fail. The moral of the poem in these terms would seem to be that of Milton's career as a political pamphleteer: no amount of instruction and admonition about ultimate truths and values will prevent the immature and inexperienced from tragic mistakes. If the angelic intellect of Raphael, God's messenger, fails to save his hearers how else could the merely human intellect of Milton fare with the English. Any trust in rational training and counsel is shown to be quite fallacious by the plausible incapacity of God himself to save his beloved creatures from corruption. This cosmic fact should also indicate how misleading is the idea that Milton wrote his poem to purge his hearers of error. If God could not do this as Milton shows, what blasphemy it would be for Milton to expect to do better! Neither the arguments nor the experience of the poem could conceivably "save" his readers from Milton's point of view without a relapse into Satanic (and Platonic) pride on his part.

For, after all, the didactic leverage that Raphael has as expositor is identical to Milton's, either as speaking necessarily (to us) in the poet's personal style, or in so far as both archangel and poet are merely the mouthpiece of the Divinity from Milton's point of view. Milton's goal must therefore be humbler insofar as he may even admit to having had a personal one in writing the epic. It is not the achievement of virtue in his audience through instruction at which he must aim, but at the clarification for his readers of what has already happened to them after a failure which it is too late for them to remedy. The purpose of the epic is therefore to make the horrid facts of the universe fully intelligible once they have been painfully learnt by experience of suffering and failure. That is why Milton's express goal in his epic is "to justify the ways of God to men," in the light of "inexplicable" failure. This cannot be to the universal advantage of all men, only of "a fit audience . . . though few" made up of those who have

suffered defeat and are willing to accept this fact to
the point of believing that they must make the best
of this oppressive outcome. Milton presents us with the
most comprehensive, vivid, and memorable discussion
of the causes, conditions, and consequences of failure
that has ever been written, above all illustrating the
positive potentialities of that sequence, after unflinchingly presenting the full horrors which the misjudgment
of failure can produce.

At the heart of the poem lies a sense that in this
ominous context what distinguishes life from death is
the inconsistency of the former, its capacity to assimilate
painful tensions and endure incompatibilities. By these
terms Satan's supposedly heroic resolution has the
rigidity not merely of neurosis but of rigor mortis:

> Farewell happy Fields
> Where Joy forever dwells: Hail horrors, hail
> Infernal world, and thou profoundest Hell
> Receive thy new Possessor: One who brings
> A mind not to be chang'd by Place or Time.
>
> (I, 249-53)

With the absolute consistency appropriate to an angelic
principle (or the perfected psychosis), Satan never de-
viates from resistance to the humiliating fact that the
rest of the universe exacts the surrender of his total
autonomy (IV, 73ff.). The elegant irony lies in the fact
that Satan is himself an absolute dictator who allows
of no significant debate by others—while the ultimate
Reality Principle itself epitomized in God the Father,
however severe in manner, actually does tolerate incompatibility and can reconcile himself to it, whether in

the Son's plea for mercy or in the modification of the apparent doom of Adam and Eve.

The paradoxical nature of the Christian Trinity has always given offense to the rigor of extreme monotheists, whether they were Platonists, Jews, or Mohammedans. But at the heart of this discontinuity lies the admonition that monolithic consistency in the vein of Plato's mode of argument is an inferior, indeed, a destructive principle which is ultimately life-opposing. How difficult it is to accept this creative discontinuity is wittily illustrated in Langland's dialogue between Peace and Righteousness in *Piers the Ploughman* (Passus XVIII) when Peace announces, "I am on my way to welcome all the lost souls whom I have not seen for many a long day now, because of the darkness of sin. For Adam and Eve and Moses and many more of those in hell are to have pardon. And oh, how I shall be dancing with joy when I see them—and you, dear sister must come and dance too." But Rightetusness replies bitterly: "Have you gone off your head? or had too much to drink! Do you really suppose that this light can unlock hell, and save the souls of men? Don't you believe it sister! God himself pronounced this Doom in the beginning, that Adam and Eve and all their seed should surely die, and after death live in torment, if ever they touched the fruit of a certain tree. In spite of this command Adam ate the fruit; so, in effect, he refused God's love as well as his law, and chose instead the word of the Devil and his wife's greed, out of all reason. I am Righteousness, and I tell you this for certain: that their suffering will never cease, and no prayer can ever help them. So leave them to the fate they chose and let us stop this argument."

However, quaintly enough, Peace insists on disagree-ing: "I can prove that their pain must come to an end, and suffering is bound to turn to happiness in the end. For if they had never known suffering, they could never know happiness.—No man can grasp what pleasure is who has never suffered, or understand hunger who has never been without food. I am sure that if there were no night, no one would know for certain the meaning of day. . . . That is why God, the creator of all things, of his goodness became a man."[5] In terms that resemble the fate of the Lady in *Comus*, Holy Church had earlier (in Passus I) warned Piers that "Chastity without charity shall lie bound in hell." On the other hand, she explains: "Heaven would not hold Love, it was so heavy in itself. But when it had eaten its fill of earth, and taken flesh and blood, then it was lighter than a leaf on a linden-tree, more subtle and piercing than the point of a needle. The strongest armour was not proof against it, the tallest ramparts could not keep it out. Therefore Love is first among the company of the Lord of Heaven."[6]

This last speech fully resolves the nature of the great battle in Milton's Heaven. It is not essentially a physical conflict designed to compete directly with the great fights in the old primary epics, which Milton fiercely repudiates as models for his discussion of the Fall:

> Sad task, yet argument
> Not less but more Heroic than the wrath
> Of stern Achilles on his Foe pursu'd
> Thrice Fugitive about Troy Wall; or rage
> Of Turnus for Lavinia disespous'd.   (IX, 13-17)

[5] Langland, *Piers the Ploughman*, trans. J. F. Goodridge (Harmonds-worth: Penguin, 1959), pp. 260-61.

[6] Goodridge, pp. 74-75.

The key to Milton's battle lies in the fact that love cannot ultimately be resisted: even raging egotism retreats before it: "the strongest armour is not proof against it." The defeat and incarceration of Satan and his followers is not a literal analogue to establishment repression of dissent, but a purely figurative model for the triumph of the mutual love of Adam and Eve over the temptation to sustained anger and suicidal despair in Book X. The Satan who is defeated in the battle in Heaven is not a wholesome or even a whole personality, but the trait of hysteria generated by affronted pride. The moral there, and in every episode in the epic, is "love conquers all":

> to create
> Is greater than created to destroy.
> Who can impair thee, mighty King, or bound
> Thy Empire? easily the proud attempt
> Of Spirits apostate and thir Counsels vain
> Thou hast repell'd, while impiously they thought
> Thee to diminish, and from thee withdraw
> The number of thy worshippers. Who seeks
> To lessen thee, against his purpose serves
> To manifest the more thy might: his evil
> Thou usest, and from thence creat'st more good.
> (VII, 604-16)

The stress on the positive and creative force epitomized by the Son requires of Milton his extended celebration of all the phases of the Creation. This is not another academic exercise in what I have called the secondary epic, but a massive characterization of the creative genius which Satan's primal egotism would seek to inhibit and extinguish; as Piers is told in Passus I: "By love, God chose to fashion all his works."[7] This deep truth underlies the whole supposedly ominous structure of the epic and only blind neurosis will deny the recurrent and conscious outcropping of this bedrock. Indeed the basic rhythm of the epic could be described as the progressive transcendence of the Satanic vision, so that from the opening in which everything is seen from a merely monomaniac (that is, diabolic) point of view, we get an increased humanizing of awareness until the reader finds himself, at last, in Wordsworth's ultimate state at Tintern Abbey:

> hearing oftentimes
> The still, sad music of humanity,
> Nor harsh nor grating, though of ample power
> To chasten and subdue.[8]

Perhaps it seems grotesque to approach the core of Milton's poem as an exquisitely framed case-analysis of fallen pride transcended—and yet this blend is precisely why it is superior both to modern tomes of clinical psychology and to merely aesthetic readings. Thus it defines the natural rhythm of spontaneous therapy in terms more vivid, convincing, and definitive than anything offered by Freud or Jung, or by any of their followers. First of all we plausibly see the world through the perfectly blinding fury of affronted pride founded on metaphysical inflexibility: the mood which none but the truly mad can sustain indefinitely. From such suicidal, self-deluding, or merely malicious shades of feeling,

[7] Goodridge, p. 74.
[8] de Selincourt, p. 207.

we progress to a rueful recognition of the deeper truths
that such moods oppose—in the dialogue in Heaven; and
thence to a careful and plausible recapitulation of how
innocence could have proceeded toward the disaster
which first precipitates pathological resentment. The
primal condition of Adam and Eve is a more sustained
version of that elusive point before Satan recognized
the challenge to his pride in the Son's creation. The
fall of Eve is identical to the Satanic pattern: resentment
at a secondary or even worse position in the celestial
hierarchy. Her motives naturally become fully clear only
after the event when she speculates about the implications of her act:

> But to *Adam* in what sort
> Shall I appear? shall I to him make known
> As yet my change, and give him to partake
> Full happiness with mee, or rather not,
> But keep the odds of Knowledge in my power
> Without Copartner? so to add what wants
> In Female Sex, the more to draw his Love,
> And render me more equal, and perhaps,
> A thing not undesirable, sometime
> Superior: for inferior who is free?
> This may be well: but what if God have seen
> And Death ensue? then I shall be no more,
> And *Adam* wedded to another *Eve*,
> Shall live with her enjoying, I extinct;
> A death to think. Confirm'd then I resolve,
> *Adam* shall share with me in bliss or woe:
> So dear I love him, that with him all deaths
> I could endure, without him live no life.

>   (IX, 816-33)

Eve here shows all the infantile egotism of the immature person who interprets every action in terms of
immediate private advantage. But even so we do not
see in her the monomaniac exclusiveness of Satan, with
his goal of metaphysically absolute dominion. He has
urged Eve to eat so that men "shall be as Gods" (IX,
708), but this is only the ultimate principle from which
Eve's decision derives. Her actual application of it has
nothing of Satan's relentless consistency in the first two
books of the poem. Her egotism may be disastrous and
potentially suicidal but it it not insane, and its application involves a far more complex assimilation of factors
than Satan requires for his satisfaction: above all a sense
of the sustaining force of love, totally missing from the
ultimate phase of neurosis epitomized in Satan, whose
nearest mood to the positive is only the desire for
community in misery (IV, 358-94).

Eve is thus a superior entity to Satan in complexity.
Like any finite thing—angel or man—she is not omniscient, and therefore must make mistakes. But since she
is not a spiritual principle, she does not need to be
absolutely rational, logical, or consistent to preserve her
identity; she will make mistakes like Satan's, but she
will not be totally governed and bound by them forever
afterwards. In Eve's reactions to Adam we see self-love,
it is true, but we also see that part of her egotism has
the happier attribute of the celestial Trinity: a wish
to be loved by that which lies outside itself, even if that
nonself may be made reassuringly inferior. Eve's speech
thus involves not only the attributes of the diabolical
Trinity: Pride, Sin, and Death, but also those of its
celestial antithesis: Love, Sacrifice, and Creativity. All

these potentialities have lain latent in Eve until this point—she has been only potentially adult and mature, that is, fully realized. The only way that her potentiality can become actual is by meeting a cathartic challenge. But it is the nature of significant challenge to enforce the recognition of otherness, both good and bad, by pain and suffering. In this speech Eve has already come through her mistake to a clearer recognition not only of her own evil tendencies, but also of her exact positive relationship to Adam: "with him all deaths I could endure."

This complex enrichment is precisely duplicated in Adam's fall, which has resulted in naive readers feeling that Adam's choice is unequivocally noble (as Eve later will assert):

> with thee
> Certain my resolution is to Die;
> For how can I live without thee, how forgo
> Thy sweet Converse and Love so dearly join'd,
> To live again in these Wild Woods forlorn?
> Should God create another *Eve*, and I
> Another Rib afford, yet loss of thee
> Would never from my heart; no no, I feel
> The Link of Nature draw me: Flesh of Flesh
> Bone of my Bone thou art, and from thy State
> Mine never shall be parted, bliss or woe.

(IX, 906-16)

One should notice that just as Adam's original desire for the creation of Eve's company for him in Paradise (VIII, 357-411) echoes humbly the Creator's own sentiments about the inadequacy of complacent solitude in

bliss, so the will to endure the miseries of that which
is less than oneself, or is indeed depraved, is a characteristic which Adam precisely shares with the Son (III,
227-40), and also with the figure of Jesus in which the
Son's choice is to be enacted via the Crucifixion. Nevertheless, if Adam's failure is subtler than Eve's ambition,
it is equally infantile: it lies not in his will to share
her miseries, but in his naive failure to analyze the
precise course of conduct likely to minimize the disaster.
Thus, for example, one does not prove one's true love
for a drunken spouse by getting intoxicated oneself, or
love for a suicidal personality by trying to kill oneself.
Adam allows his immature flood of feeling to sweep him
into false responses, flattering Eve not so much by his
concern for her as by his extravagance in error, an
extravagance reflected in her own flamboyant response:

> O glorious trial of exceeding Love,
> Illustrious evidence, example high!
> Ingaging me to emulate, but short
> Of thy perfection, how shall I attain,
> *Adam*, from whose dear side I boast me sprung,
> And gladly of our Union hear thee speak,
> One Heart, one Soul in both; whereof good proof
> This day affords, declaring thee resolv'd,
> Rather then Death or aught than Death more dread
> Shall separate us, linkt in Love so dear,
> To undergo with mee one Guilt, one Crime.
>
> (IX, 961-71)

Perhaps the neatest illustration of the immature folly
of these sentimental idealizations of invalid choices lies
in reminding ourselves that it is by exactly these enthusiastic misjudgments of the facts that Romeo and Juliet

(not to mention Pyramus and Thisbe) destroy themselves needlessly.

The incorrectness of Adam's too hectic choice becomes apparent as soon as the depressive phase succeeds, in the manic-depressive cycle to which he has committed himself. The letdown from ecstasy is always at least equal to the previous "high," by some psychological equivalent to Newton's Third Law of Motion. Far from sustaining their unnatural enthusiasm, Adam and Eve fall to diabolic attitudes recapitulating those of Satan's cohorts in the debate in Hell in Book II, progressing from Moloch's wrathfulness to the suicidal plans of Eve in Book X. We see in full detail the realistic psychology of which the Battle in Heaven and the rest of the career of Satan were the archetypes. But the core truth is that the knowledge of those archetypes in a purely intellectual form is practically useless. Until knowledge has been tested on our pulses it has no mental force. Thus the moral of *Paradise Lost* is not to "beware of Satan's enormous charms," for it shows rather that it is useless merely to know of them academically. As consciously fallen people, Milton does not expect us naively to side with Satan once more in his epic; but he no more expects us to avoid failure in the future merely by studying Adam and Eve than they could by studying Satan's fall under Raphael's tutorship. Again, Milton's goal must be far less ambitious: to help us confirm intellectually what we have already tragically and truly learned from experience, "to justify the ways of God to men"—in other words to explain how a providential deity might allow the misery into which it seems that we have irreversibly betrayed ourselves.

The essential point is nevertheless in part a classical one: that suffering is the only true education, or as Aeschylus phrases it, "Zeus has ordained that man through suffering shall learn." But in Milton's Christian vision the value of the knowledge always ultimately outweighs the suffering, however horrendous. *Paradise Lost* is not the confident "comedy" of Dante because there is no sense of the definitive attainment of a point of absolute rest such as climaxes *The Divine Comedy*, and because initially the terrible cost of *any* advance appears intolerable.

In Milton we are faced with an endless and deeply agonizing series of failures, each resulting in a wrenching realignment which, in the end, proves demonstrably superior to the previous one, and a worthy compensation for the dreadful losses and suffering it costs. In Milton's epic, Adam and Eve (and the reader equally) are invited to reappraise continuously the adequacy of the best that has previously been known to the rationalizing mind of Plato's type. From primal darkness and unawareness rises first the flaming egotism of infantile being: solipsistic and totally self-involved. This is succeeded in turn by a genuine if dramatic duality, resulting from a conscious self-division, which proves far more versatile than the primitive consistency and self-sufficiency, though at first far less flamboyant and absolute. Elemental consistency is thus irreversibly repudiated as a religious, psychological, social, or ethical principle, and with it the monolithic rationalism of Plato, in favor of something discontinuous, costly, and unpredictable, but always evolving. Thus the fall of Satan and the resulting remedial creation of Man is a progression from philosophic monism to something beyond systematic analysis, for which only the subtlest work of art can stand as model, serving in its complex discontinuities as a concrete universal, or objective correlative for humanity, a model which we may rationalize from what we have experienced, but whose nature we can no more predict in advance than we can our own futures.

Obviously, in such a universe the shallow, affective methods of the pamphleteer and the rhetorician are ridiculous irrelevancies: they emphatically cannot valuably affect people's behavior by rational argument or emotional tricks. At best the rational mind may hope only to explain why things have already gone wrong, well after the event. In *Paradise Lost* only Michael, endowed with God's foresight, may significantly clarify Adam's future for him; but even this derives only from Milton's own hindsight of past events and affords no helpful advice to the reader—as Adam realizes:

Let no man seek

Henceforth to be foretold what shall befall
Him or his Children, evil he may be sure,
Which neither his foreknowing can prevent,
And hee the future evil shall no less
In apprehension than in substance feel
Grievous to bear.

(XI, 770-76)

How different this is from the vision of England's future with which Milton had concluded *Areopagitica*, and had even, incredibly, reasserted as late as 1660 in *A Ready and Easy Way to Establish a Free Commonwealth*!

Yet Adam is never left in this agonized mood. He is continually forced to revise his criteria of judgment, initially to his cost, but always to his ultimate advantage:

> O thou who future things canst represent
> As present, Heav'nly instructor, I revive
> At this last sight, assur'd that Man shall live
> With all the Creatures, and thir seed preserve.
> Far less I now lament for one whole World
> Of wicked Sons destroy'd, than I rejoice
> For one Man found so perfet and so just,
> That God voutsafes to raise another World
> From him, and all his anger to forget.
>
> (XI, 870-78)

Each cycle of suffering raises Adam to a marginally higher level of awareness, until as the archetype of humanity by anticipation he is blessed with the full range of experience of the Christian era of Milton and his readers, whose understanding he attains through the operation of Michael's angelic intelligence:

> So Law appears imperfet, and but giv'n
> With purpose to resign them in full time
> Up to a better Cov'nant, disciplin'd
> From shadowy Types to Truth, from Flesh to Spirit,
> From imposition of strict Laws, to free
> Acceptance of large Grace, from servile fear
> To filial, works of Law to works of Faith.
>
> (XII, 300-06)

In the observation of the mere event, Adam finally grasps what the virtuoso yet purely academic instruction of Raphael had failed to achieve fully: "now clear I understand / What oft my steadiest thoughts have searcht in vain" (XII, 376-7). Steady thought of the kind

Raphael developed in Adam (VIII, 179-97) is a useless guide to future behavior, because the actual future is never predictable, involving as it does new experiences, fresh awareness, and satisfactions transcending their cost—however intolerable this cost may be by any known (and hence archaic) values. Such a paradoxical recognition of the inevitability and value of failure is the cornerstone of the work, expressed consciously in Adam's classic exclamation on the theme of *felix culpa*:

> O goodness infinite, goodness immense!
> That all this good of evil shall produce,
> And evil turn to good; more wonderful
> Than that which by creation first brought forth
> Light out of darkness! full of doubt I stand,
> Whether I should repent me now of sin
> By mee done and occasion'd, or rejoice
> Much more, that much more good thereof shall spring,
> To God more glory, more good will to Men
> From God, and over wrath grace shall abound.
>
>   (XII, 469-78)

This sentiment is impossible in a Platonic state, where the mere mention of failure by the poets is sufficient to invite their exile. It is ironic that in *The Republic* Socrates is made to threaten those who even talk of evil with expulsion from the womb of the city-state, but that the mature Milton's sympathy at the end of his epic lies not with the ruined Eden which Adam and Eve must leave, but with their own newly born condition as happily autonomous adults:

> The World was all before them, where to choose
> Thir place of rest, and Providence thir guide.
>
>   (XII, 646-7)

The dream of plausibly reforming England into an ideal and exemplary state almost destroyed Milton, not to mention its dislocation of his mind. The contemplation of Man's irremediable incompetence by contrast seems to leave him confident of the future, however costly the coming of that future might prove to be. It remained for Milton to display the possible Christian role in that evolution.

6: The Christian Revolutionary

The Existential Ethic of *Paradise Regained*

The sense of omnipotence reflected in the writings of the youthful Milton and the sense of failure in those of his maturity are almost universal experiences. Any gifted person fostered by a favorable environment is likely to first share this sense of unlimited potentiality, and then assimilate the humiliating shock of reality as the world fails to match his expectations. The two last major works of Milton explore these extreme limits of mental experience which are nearly inevitable for the most gifted: the correct self-definition of excellence as it anticipates the future, and the redeployment in the face of failure to which even the best are exposed. As the biographical parallels between his own life and that of each of the heroes indicates, these are extremes which Milton himself underwent more than once, and they cover the full range of human awareness from abject physical and mental ruin to the confident demonstration of divine endowment.

The extraordinary fact about the two poems is that, starting from opposite ends of the mental spectrum with

the Son of God and the dupe of Dalila, Milton con-
clusively shows that the mental discipline preparatory to decisive action in each case requires total repudiation of rational prediction. In attempting to change
the course of human history, Milton's heroes are initially
forced to adopt a posture not merely of total skepticism,
but of a complete passivity which even the professed
skeptic rarely attains. This stasis is only the significant
prelude to events which permanently alter the established order; but nevertheless it is the precondition of
the success of the heroes that they should reject ambitious egotism by first standing absolutely still, stripped
of personal thoughts, premeditated goals, and any co-
herent ideological relationship. In rejecting premeditated achievement and sustained philosophy, Milton's two
last works involve a repudiation and total dismantling
of most of what Western culture has derived from either
of the two great sources of ratiocination in the Greek
tradition, Plato and Aristotle. The poems are a reaffir-
mation of the supremacy of what primitive Christians
might call the will of God as opposed to the will of
man. St. Paul wrote: "If any man among you think
himself one of the world's clever ones, let him discard
his cleverness that he may learn to be truly wise. For
this world's cleverness is stupidity to God" (1 Corinthians, 3.18-9; Phillips' translation).

In these terms *Paradise Regained* is a total survey
of all those goals which well-meaning men propose as
the proper concern of the exceptionally gifted. And in
this context, we should hesitate to take a naive view
of the Devil's role in this poem. If modern critics have
tended to exaggerate the attractions which even hind-

sight must allow to the Satan of *Paradise Lost*, they have equally tended to minimize the substantial virtues of the Devil of *Paradise Regained*. After all, the poem deals with the temptation of the most perfect of men, and the Devil himself ridicules crude proposals like that of his cohort Belial—to deflect Jesus into sexual adventures. This kind of sensuality might serve to damage an Achilles, or an Æneas, but not the Christ. The only temptations possible in this case are such as might plausibly enter the mind of the best of men, conscious of great virtues and of the obligation to use them to the highest ends. Inevitably therefore the Devil of *Paradise Regained* is not the exponent of a vulgar and potentially pathological evil of the kind accurately portrayed in *Paradise Lost*. Indeed, by conventional standards his proposals are not evil at all, except in the sense that anything less than perfection can be called such.

With this in mind, we must consider Christ's Devil as morally superior to any other diabolic force. To use our modern terminology, he represents the mental forces working not for vice or crime but against the fullest self-realization, and such pressures are only those which complete virtue might plausibly recognize. If this Devil is equated with the libidinal drives of the uniquely excellent psyche, then he can only propose courses which are, of themselves, completely worthy and universally defined as good by any rational standards. The dialogue between Jesus and his tempter can therefore be considered in a very specific and positive sense as a dialogue in the mind of Jesus, not so much between naive good and crude evil but between one kind of virtue and another normally held to be such. The poem is from the start concerned to establish that the locus of the confrontations is not so much an objective place but a mind, and the core of the poem can be considered "a dialogue of one" in Donne's useful phrase. What we discover is an archetypal example of the self-analysis which devout Freudians limit to their Master in his initial psychoanalysis of himself; but Milton lays out the whole procedure with a definitiveness and comprehensiveness that no mere psychoanalyst has yet attained.

From the start Jesus rejects received opinions, motives, and methods. The poem's structure essentially illustrates a technique for unravelling the conditioned responses of the mind. It suits Milton's purposes to show that Jesus is not consciously possessed of supernatural powers at this point in his career, and his mind is apparently human in its resources, giving him an enhanced exemplary value to ordinary readers. If some kind of divine sanction describes Jesus as a "perfect Man, by Merit call'd my Son" (I, 166), it is also a recognition which the youthful Milton came close to proclaiming for himself in the personal asides of his prose pamphlets. In the account of the youthful Jesus, we may possibly recognize a conscious parallelism to what we read of Milton's description of his own studious childhood in *The Second Defence* (see pp. 33-34):

> When I was yet a child, no childish play
> To me was pleasing, all my mind was set
> Serious to learn and know and thence to do
> What might be public good; myself I thought
> Born to that end.   (I, 201-5)

This precise psychological touch is less important for any provable identity with Milton's life than because it illustrates a plausible mental condition for any "infant prodigy." In starting his "retreat" Jesus does not have any confident sense of his own ultimate role beyond that normally available to human consciousness. If anything, he starts out in an exceptional state of uncertainty—all he feels is a strong desire for solitude:

And now by some strong motion I am led
Into this Wilderness, to what intent
I learn not yet; perhaps I need not know;
For what concerns my knowledge God reveals.

(I, 290-3)

In this condition we perceive a complete rejection of ratiocinative procedures and the *a priori* approach to decision making which has been associated with Plato. The only mental attributes strongly present here are readiness and responsiveness, without any predetermined frame of reference such as lurks behind even the affected uncertainties of Socratic dialectic.

In *Renaissance Landscapes*[1] I have elaborately detailed the catalytic effect which rural solitude is traditionally supposed to have on human psychology, and here it will suffice to suggest that what Jesus does in his fasting withdrawal from human society is to prepare the mental ground for a psychomachia, or "self-analysis" by some simple and traditional but effective physical techniques, for which the modern use of "mind-expanding" drugs is a pathetically inadequate and dangerous

[1] H. M. Richmond, *Renaissance Landscapes: English Poems in a European Tradition* (The Hague: Mouton, 1973).

alternative. It is quite natural to note that Jesus experiences the modest entrancement described by the sensitive young intellectual in *L'Allegro* and *Il Penseroso*:

> Thus wore out night, and now the Herald Lark
> Left his ground-nest, high tow'ring to descry
> The morn's approach, and greet her with his Song.
> As lightly from his grassy Couch up rose
> Our Savior, and found all was but a dream,
> Fasting he went to sleep, and fasting wak'd.
> Up to a hill anon his steps he rear'd,
> From whose high top to ken the prospect round,
> If Cottage were in view, Sheepcote or Herd;
> But Cottage, Herd or Sheepcote none he saw,
> Only in bottom saw a pleasant Grove,
> With chant of tuneful Birds resounding loud.
> Thither he went his way, determin'd there
> To rest at noon, and enter'd soon the shade
> High rooft, and walks beneath, and alleys brown
> That open'd in the midst a woody Scene;
> Nature's own work it seem'd (Nature taught Art)
> And to a superstitious eye the haunt
> Of Wood Gods and Wood Nymphs; he view'd it round,
> When suddenly a man before him stood.

(II, 279-98)

Each appearance and disappearance of the Devil stresses his hallucinatory character, which is the natural result of the attenuated physical vigor of Jesus. And each of the Devil's arguments does not rise from an alien personality but from the logic of the immediate circumstances of Jesus, which naturally afford the bases of each argument. Thus the very first temptation arises from the universal physical needs stressed by the life in the Wilderness which Jesus is temporarily sharing:

> we here
> Live on tough roots and stubs, to thirst inur'd
> More than the Camel, and to drink go far,
> Men to much misery and hardship born;
> But if thou be the Son of God, Command
> That out of these hard stones be made thee Bread;
> So shalt thou save thyself and us relieve
> With Food, whereof we wretched seldom taste.
>
> (I, 338-45)

The idea is a natural and proper one: a man of talent's first instinct is to devote himself to the means for survival, not only for himself of course, but for the well being of the whole community. It is a choice that many worthy minds have made, from "the Father of the Green Revolution" down to the lowliest member of the Peace Corps, Vista, or the OEO programs. Helping the poor to become productive is an almost irresistible argument to well-meaning modern youth; but the question must still at least be asked: "Is sheer physical productivity the best goal for humane genius?" Even more today, environmentalists and "futurologists" strongly question the ultimate value of material gain, and thus the next natural step in the dialogue of the self must be to ask how far one's estimates of the future do justify pursuing immediately satisfying physical goals. Such use of one's genius for skilled prediction is readily rationalized as a blessing. It might be Dr. Gallup himself speaking:

> Men generally think me much a foe
> To all mankind: why should I? they to me

> Never did wrong or violence; by them
> I lost not what I lost, rather by them
> I gain'd what I have gain'd, and with them dwell
> Copartner in these Regions of the World,
> If not disposer; lend them oft my aid,
> Oft my advice by presages and signs,
> And answers, oracles, portents and dreams,
> Whereby they may direct their future life.
>
> (I, 387-96)

The reply is equally modern, for the Devil is warned that, while "God hath justly giv'n the Nations up / To thy Delusions" because of their volatility, the futur-ologist is rarely in business for other people's good: personal profit and prejudice are powerfully distorting factors, and from the time of Job to that of Ho Chi Minh the underdog's endurance has often falsified pre-dictions, however plausible. Most of the debates about long-term policy prove as false as the exponential growth rates that used to govern graphs for population and productivity, and that now reappear in apocalyptic forecasts of pollution rates and the exhausting of natural resources.

His superiority to elementary motivations proved, Jesus has vindicated his sophistication sufficiently to merit full celebrity treatment—to be invited out to urbane but expensive gatherings, where he may savor gourmet cooking, ogle fashionable beauties, and share high cultural connections (II, 336-77). When Jesus reacts contemptuously to this flattering possibility, the Devil is forced back on practical politics as a serious subject to offset the embarrassing frivolity which this bluntness identifies in his offers. After all, it is quite obvious that

even a charismatic political leader from the lower classes
does need a financial base, or at least a wealthy sponsor,
if he is to get any real results:

> all thy heart is set on high designs,
> High actions; but wherewith to be achiev'd?
> Great acts require great means of enterprise;
> Thou art unknown, unfriended, low of birth,
> A Carpenter thy Father known, thyself
> Bred up in poverty and straits at home;
> Lost in a Desert here and hunger-bit:
> Which way or from what hope dost thou aspire
> To greatness? Whence Authority deriv'st,
> What Followers, what Retinue canst thou gain,
> Or at thy heels the dizzy Multitude
> Longer than thou canst feed them on thy cost? . . .
> Therefore, if at great things thou wouldst arrive,
> Get Riches first, get Wealth, and Treasure heap,
> Not difficult, if thou hearken to me,
> Riches are mine, Fortune is in my hand.

(II, 410-21, 426-9)

The argument is not facile: Schliemann's heroic
triumphs in archeology were founded on a successful
career as a businessman; the Medici were originally
bankers; even Plato and Milton themselves had private
means on which they depended for their freedom to
pursue their careers. But the answer is almost too easy
for Jesus: that a man with a genuine cause always makes
his mark, and to distort one's views about it in order
to court popularity risks destroying the most powerful
resources of a potential reformer: the inner harmony
of conscious integrity, and the public reputation of
unflinchingly pursuing "the way of truth."

Clearly then, logic suggests the need to begin the campaign at once, to get the issues out into the open and so establish oneself as a rallying point for enthusiastic support:

These Godlike Virtues wherefore dost thou hide?
Affecting private life, or more obscure
In savage Wilderness, wherefore deprive
All Earth her wonder at thy acts, thyself
The fame and glory, glory the reward
That sole excites to high attempts the flame
Of most erected Spirits.

(III, 21-27)

Yet the risk of debasement by overexposure to facile responses is one of the most ominous threats to gifted intellects of every era. It is not merely in our own Age of Publicity that the misinformed public may be censured because "they praise and they admire they know not what; / And know not whom." The real test of distinction and worth lies with the man "who dares be singularly good," for to maintain the right when the world is against one is the mark of the true hero. And now we are getting close to the paradoxical core of the poem, for Temptation next simply exposes the implicit logic of Jesus' last reply: in any campaign, commitment is more important than finances, publicity, or political leverage:

If Kingdom move thee not, let move thee Zeal
And Duty; Zeal and Duty are not slow,
But on Occasion's forelock watchful wait.
They themselves rather are occasion best,
Zeal of thy Father's house, Duty to free

Thy Country from her Heathen servitude;
So shalt thou best fullfil, best verify
The Prophets old.

(III, 171-78)

One notes that these are precisely the choices made by
the immature Milton: to seek zealously for the reform
of religion and the liberation of England from tyranny.
However, the sweeping terms and vagueness of the
enterprise are self-evident, and they are susceptible to
the same critique to which Popper submits Plato's
utopianism.

The alternative is to learn competence by localized
mistakes which are instructive but not costly and irre-
versible, however humiliating they may seem:

What if [God] hath decreed that I shall first
Be tried in humble state, and things adverse,
By tribulations, injuries, insults,
Contempts, and scorns, and snares, and violence,
Suffering, abstaining, quietly expecting
Without distrust or doubt, that he may know
What I can suffer, how obey? who best
Can suffer, best can do; best reign, who first
Well hath obey'd; just trial e'er I merit
My exaltation without change or end.

(III, 188-97)

Yet nagging doubts persist: can one be sure of one's
identity without some dramatic demonstration, seeking
what Satan calls

My harbor and my ultimate repose,
The end I would attain, my final good. . . .
Why move thy feet so slow to what is best,

> Happiest both to thyself and all the world
> That thou who worthiest art shouldst be thir King?
> (III, 210-11, 224-26)

It is significant that Jesus makes no reply to this question which racked Milton at every phase of his career (remember the sonnet "How soon hath time"). To stand coolly by watching disasters and the suffering and misery they produce cannot be directly justified in principle. But it can be answered in practice by recognizing a further problem: granted the will to help, what certain means can one take without risk of worsening the issue?

This consideration leads to the climax of the poem, the discussion of what resources are available to affect the human condition. The simplest and most traditional is military force, and it is the role of Assyria to illustrate this approach. As successful resisters to the might of Imperial Rome, the armies of Assyria may properly stand for the vindication of national identity by legitimate warfare. Nor need this be a method which repudiates the Law (as modern Israel would agree), as is shown by the reference to Cyrus (III, 284) whose military prowess was compatible with liberation of the Jews. The supreme Jewish precedent, of course, is David himself:

> thy Kingdom though foretold
> By Prophet or by Angel, unless thou
> Endeavor, as thy Father *David* did,
> Thou never shalt obtain; prediction still
> In all things, and all men, supposes means,
> Without means us'd, what it predicts revokes.
> (III, 351-56)

Yet implicit in this choice is a narrowness of vision, for it is a vindication of a single nation, a single ethnic tradition, or a single race, against the rest of humanity. If one vindicates oneself at the expense of others, this in turn invites the relentless scrutiny of one's own tradition and its debatable claims to supremacy. At the end of Book III Jesus turns on the Hebrew tradition the same hostile scrutiny that the aging Milton directed at the English from whom he had once hoped so much would come in concluding *Areopagitica*.

One is left then only with non-ethnic means: the international approach—and the only international institution available in the lifetime of Jesus was Imperial Rome, by broad if not unanimous consent the high point of Western society in its laws, organization, and manners. If Practical Reason was to afford a cultural image for itself to Milton, Rome alone could serve, for probably no single integrated society has more fully determined Western culture's physical character and social organization. Most of our political terms and nearly all of our legal ones derive from Rome. Only the highest flights of rhetoric can do justice to the best that Rome still represents, and Milton's expository style reaches its ultimate perfection in the great speech evoking the architectural and administrative magnificence of Rome (IV, 25-89). Moreover, it is to be taken at face value. Scholars who wrangle about why Milton sets this praise of Rome in the Devil's mouth misjudge the case if they think we are to reject the praise as merely false. Rome did confer great blessings on its empire: Gibbon even felt that under the Antonine emperors mankind reached its peak of happiness in all of recorded history. To rectify

the running of such a vast instrument for the organization of mankind's well-being is a choice few of us could
censure, reserving as we do our highest admiration for
that man who has the courage and talent to undertake
such a challenge. It is a burden which only a very few
exceptional men can carry with even moderate success,
as the Devil's allusions to the degeneracy and ineffi-
ciency of Tiberius remind us, and here again we run
into complications.

If high office is so rarely well handled, that role is
at best an uncertain source of achievement for the
individual to consider. The failures of powerful men
must remind us that all mankind is fallible; even the
best cannot avert human error because institutions
cannot impose virtue and happiness from without. The
ultimate problem is thus not social reform, but mental
restoration, as Jesus ripostes to the Devil:

> [thou] proceed'st to talk
> Of the Emperor, how easily subdu'd
> How gloriously; I shall, thou say'st, expel
> A brutish monster; what if I withal
> Expel a Devil who first made him such?
> Let his tormentor Conscience find him out;
> For him I was not sent, nor yet to free
> That people victor once, now vile and base,
> Deservedly made vassal.

(IV, 125-33)

And so we come at last face to face with Plato again,
in the Devil's last plea: if applied reason is a vain hope,
the training and reform of the mind must be one's
method; and for this ultimate procedure the plausible
epitome is Athens and its intellectual life.

Let me say at this point that the conventional dispraise of the more sober style of *Paradise Regained* as uniformly inferior to the flamboyant vein of *Paradise Lost* seems to me exactly wrong. The decorous economy of the short epic illustrates a far higher aesthetic achievement, covering as it does equally the whole range of human awareness and performance, and rising, as it does in the praise of Athens, to the greatest passage of verse that Milton ever wrote:

Look once more ere we leave this specular Mount
Westward, much nearer by Southwest, behold
Where on the *Aegean* shore a City stands
Built nobly, pure the air, and light the soil,
Athens, the eye of *Greece*, Mother of Arts
And Eloquence, native to famous wits
Or hospitable, in her sweet recess,
City or Suburban, studious walks and shades;
See there the Olive Grove of *Academe*,
Plato's retirement, where the *Attic* Bird
Trills her thick-warbl'd notes the summer long;
There flow'ry hill *Hymettus* with the sound
Of Bees' industrious murmur oft invites
To studious musing; there *Ilissus* rolls
His whispering stream; within the walls then view
The schools of ancient Sages; his who bred
Great *Alexander* to subdue the world,
Lyceum there, and painted *Stoa* next;
There thou shalt hear and learn the secret power
Of harmony in tones and numbers hit
By voice or hand, and various-measur'd verse,
Aeolian charms and *Dorian* Lyric Odes,
And his who gave them breath, but higher sung,

Blind *Melesigenes* thence *Homer* call'd,
Whose Poem *Phoebus* challeng'd for his own.
Thence what the lofty grave Tragedians taught
In *Chorus* or *Iambic*, teachers best
Of moral prudence, with delight receiv'd
In brief sententious precepts, while they treat
Of fate, and chance, and change in human life,
High actions, and high passions best describing:
Thence to the famous Orators repair,
Those ancient, whose resistless eloquence
Wielded at will that fierce Democraty,
Shook the Arsenal and fulmin'd over *Greece*,
To *Macedon*, and *Artaxerxes'* Throne;
To sage Philosophy next lend thine ear,
From Heaven descended to the low-rooft house
Of *Socrates*, see there his Tenement,
Whom well inspir'd the Oracle pronounc'd
Wisest of men; from whose mouth issu'd forth
Mellifluous streams that water'd all the schools
Of Academics old and new, with those
Surnam'd *Peripatetics*, and the Sect
Epicurean, and the *Stoic* severe;
These here revolve, or, as thou lik'st, at home,
Till time mature thee to a Kingdom's weight;
These rules will render thee a King complete
Within thyself, much more with Empire join'd.
                                        .   (IV, 236-84)

Here the whole range of human intellectual activity
is evoked; the urbane manners, aesthetic sophistication,
and intellectual virtuosity of Athens may properly stand
for all that is distinguished in the performance of the
human intellect, and it is very important to observe

that Milton makes Jesus recognize these experiences as
a proper part of his own mind: "Think not but that
I know these things" (IV, 286). But the high intellectual
life is no more exempt from moral failure than the
statesman's, general's, or patriot's. Jesus observes that
the philosopher is just as capable of shallow vanity and
egotism as the next man, and that even in his professional discipline his effective goal is self-aggrandisement.
Nor is learning in the least a guarantee of wisdom:

>   many books
> Wise men have said are wearisome; who reads
> Incessantly, and to his reading brings not
> A spirit and judgment equal or superior
> (And what he brings, what need he elsewhere seek)
> Uncertain and unsettl'd still remains,
> Deep verst in books and shallow in himself,
> Crude or intoxicate, collecting toys,
> And trifles for choice matters, worth a sponge;
> As Children gathering pebbles on the shore.
>   (IV, 321-30)

No wonder this reply has distressed modern humanists.
Its rejection of academic values as well as Academic
ones cuts too close to the heart of criticism and scholarship itself. The whole life of the intellect enshrined in
university education on the Platonic model is here
repudiated. Among true philosophers, the only point
about using ratiocinative skills is to discredit them:

> The first and wisest of them all profess'd
> To know this only, that he nothing knew.
>   (IV, 293-94)

This rejection of systematic thinking is not only the ultimate reaction of Jesus to Western culture in so far as it derives from the pagan classics, it reflects the considered and hostile verdict of Milton on that tradition as a source of reform and progress after a lifetime spent in its application to England—a lifetime now crowned with a failure as total as that of Plato himself in Syracuse. Inevitably, every conventional motive for public action is falsified by events which unexpectedly reverse one's expectations, as almost all tragic drama illustrates in seeking to epitomize history. In such circumstances, what does the scrupulous but well-meaning personality consciously choose to do? Only one defensible answer is possible: nothing significant. It is a terribly costly and humiliating reply, and the Devil's contemptuous response is one that such a decision invites even in the very person who makes the choice:

> Since neither wealth, nor honor, arms nor arts,
> Kingdom nor Empire pleases thee, nor aught
> By me propos'd in life contemplative,
> Or active, tended on by glory, or fame,
> What dost thou in this World? The Wilderness
> For thee is fittest place.

(IV, 368-73)

Of course, Jesus does provide an alternative source of motivation which might require the pursuit of *any* of these rejected means *if* the Will of God should oblige him to do so:

>   he who receives
> Light from above, from the fountain of light,
> No other doctrine needs, though granted true. . . .
> Where God is prais'd aright, and Godlike men,

The Holiest of Holies, and his Saints;
Such are from God inspir'd.

(IV, 288-90, 348-50)

And how does one know the voice of God when one hears it? The poem's first, pragmatic answer is that one can ruefully assume that one scarcely ever will hear it: the cosmic imperative is not a chatterbox. If Christ himself can find no divinely sanctioned course of conduct for the salvation of men, it is scarcely likely that lesser mortals will be continually afforded legitimate and salutary choices. The first step on encountering a compelling motive for action is to apply the *argumentum ad hominem* firmly and subtly to oneself. Very little objective validity remains thereafter in most decisions, as Robert Frost reminds us in "The Road Not Taken."

The mark of true self-knowledge for the aging Milton is the fullest recognition of the meaning of that famous conclusion to his sonnet: "They also serve who only stand and wait." When that was first written, it seemed the necessary self-consolation of a blind man, but now it appears the archetypal awareness of the wise. For such a person the highest purely humane achievement becomes mastery of the art of standing perfectly still.

Nor is this so trivial an achievement. Even the mere muscular poise required to stand still is possessed by few and is universally held to be the distinctive prerequisite of military prowess. The British guardsman who faints on parade is subject to punishment for his inadequacy; the fighter pilots who won the Battle of Britain (some after voting, or approving the famous motion at the Oxford Union that they would "not fight for King and Country"), also had to pass a preliminary test of balancing a pencil standing on its end at the tip of a ruler held at arm's length. Conversely, when Shakespeare wishes to discredit the character of Brutus, he does it by stressing his hastiness of movement in battle: "Brutus gave the word too early." (*Julius Caesar*, V.iii.5) For more than mere muscular poise is involved in physical balance: the human body remains still not by passivity, but by incessant minute corrections of stance depending on the fullest sensory alertness and intuitive awareness. We are now all psychiatrists enough to note our neighbor's twitches as symptoms of nervousness, if not neurosis. In a famous episode in Fitzgerald's *Tender is the Night*, the hero a little wryly but ominously vindicates his superior mental resources by drawing the attention of his friends at a bar to the fact that he alone in the entire gathering is devoid of the little eccentric movements by which all the room's other occupants betray their mental unbalance. But of course, as his name indicates, Dick Diver is susceptible to the ultimate failure that Milton's Christ avoids: Diver is destroyed and his power for good sterilized because his loving desire to save the mind of a disturbed woman extends his professional role beyond the limits of wise detachment—hence his fall.

By contrast, Christ triumphantly passes the final test of the Devil, when he is put on "the highest Pinnacle" of the Temple (IV, 549): "There stand, if thou wilt stand; to stand upright / Will ask thee skill" (IV, 551-52). The test is supremely subtle—it absolutely invites disaster from the smallest involuntary movement or any ambitious thought which might cause it; but Christ is utterly poised as the Devil has already testified:

> opportunity I here have had
> To try thee, sift thee, and confess have found thee
> Proof against all temptation as a rock
> Of Adamant, and as a Center, firm:
> To th' utmost of mere man both wise and good,
> Not more; for Honors, Riches, Kingdoms, Glory
> Have been before contemn'd, and may again.
>
> (IV, 531-37)

Christ stands firm, while it is the potential neuroses that the Devil epitomizes which prove instable and fall. Yet nothing beyond simple survival, by standing still, reflects Christ's achievement; and in the absence of any sense of God's will for him, "hee unobserv'd / Home to his Mother's house private return'd." (IV, 638-39)

Since I have been censorious about Plato, it is only fair to note that even he questions the ultimate power of reason by his climactic recourse to myth and fiction in so many of his dialogues. The most famous of these stories is that with which *The Republic* concludes, in which the wise Odysseus is described after his death as choosing the fate for his next incarnation. Others had hastily chosen lives of apparent distinction which proved painful in the event because each "had not carefully examined every point before making his choice. . . . It so happened that the soul of Odysseus had drawn the last lot of all. When he came up to choose, the memory of his former sufferings had so abated his ambition, that he went about a long time looking for a quiet retired life, which with great trouble he discovered lying about, and thrown contemptuously aside by others. As soon as he saw it, he chose it gladly, and said that he would have done the same, if he had even

drawn the first lot" (X, 614-21).[2] Thus ironically, the
climax of *The Republic* itself swerves into mere quietism,
after all its grandiose speculations about the ideal state.
However, paradoxically, the same effect in *Paradise
Regained* is seen as only a prelude to the most decisive
of human careers, one which has permanently altered
human consciousness and the human condition. For
Plato, standing still is the rueful conclusion to an
intellectually and politically ambitious career; for the
mature Milton such a condition is the necessary prerequisite for beginning a decisive achievement.

Samson Agonistes: The Existential Act

Paradise Regained achieves an epic synthesis of material as widely diversified as *Paradise Lost*, but the
longer work focusses its encyclopedic lore on the com-
mission of an archetypal error, the shorter epic on the
state of mind which offsets such a mistake. While the
more subjective focus is closer to our modern overriding
concern with subjective personality, the fact remains
that (as in *The Passion*) in *Paradise Regained* Milton
has stopped short of the painful climax of tragic suffering, the physical crucifixion of Christ and the accompan-
ying dreadful loss of confidence (which vindicates Milton's sense of Christ's limited human consciousness:
"My God, why did you forsake me?" Mark, 15,34;
Phillips). In a sense the Christ with whom Milton
presents us in *Paradise Regained* remains the master
of dialectic which Platonic tradition would predicate as
the foundation of virtue. True, the ultimate model

[2] Plato, *The Republic*, trans. J. L. Davies (London: Macmillan, 1950),
p. 369.

antedates Plato, for Christ's skepticism of conventional success finds some valid and admitted precedent in the attitudes of Socrates, who trusted his irrational *daemon* far more than Plato would have done. However, Christ, as a uniquely gifted person, serves as the supreme example in the regulation and repudiation of traditional knowledge, but by that very fact he necessarily exceeds the normal capacity. It is the mark of Milton's power to complete the range of his survey of human experience that, from the archetypal roles of Adam and Christ, he can move to the presentation of a highly particularized and conspicuously fallible illustration of human behavior in Samson's career—yet one which corroborates the point of view of Milton's maturity which was reflected equally in his Christ.

The opening of the play is almost identical in conception to the initiation of Christ's expedition into the Wilderness. The providential inspiration to seek out the catalytic psychological effect of rural solitude is offered to both heroes:

A little onward lend thy guiding hand
To these dark steps, a little further on;
For yonder bank hath choice of Sun or Shade, . . .
Retiring from the popular noise, I seek
This unfrequented place to find some ease;
Ease to the body some, none to the mind
From restless thoughts, that like a deadly swarm
Of Hornets arm'd, no sooner found alone,
But rush upon me thronging, and present
Times past, what once I was, and what I am now.

(1-3, 16-22)

One recalls how the Lady was similarly exposed to the libidinal powers of Comus by isolation in "single darkness":

> A thousand fantasies
> Begin to throng into my memory
> Of calling shapes and beck'ning shadows dire,
> And airy tongues that syllable men's names
> On Sands and Shores and desert Wildernesses.
>
> (205-9)

But the Lady's naive virtue complacently assumes her safety in the face of such threats. Samson has no such assurance, and his physical and mental circumstances parallel if not exceed the Stygian darkness in which we first find the Satan of *Paradise Lost*:

> Blind among enemies, O worse than chains,
> Dungeon, or beggary, or decrepit age!
> Light the prime work of God to me is extinct,
> And all her various objects of delight
> Annull'd, which might in part my grief have eas'd,
> Inferior to the vilest now become
> Of man or worm; the vilest here excel me,
> They creep, yet see; I dark in light expos'd
> To daily fraud, contempt, abuse, and wrong,
> Within doors, or without, still as a fool,
> In power of others, never in my own;
> Scarce half I seem to live, dead more than half.
> O dark, dark, dark, amid the blaze of noon,
> Irrecoverably dark, total Eclipse
> Without all hope of day!
>
> (68-82)

Nor does he show Satan's fixed sense of injured merit, but despairingly asks: "Whom have I to complain of but myself?" as he recognizes his own "impotence of mind" in surrendering his heroic power "weakly to a woman" and thus admits that he is "not made to rule / But to subserve." (46-57)

By Platonic or even Aristotelian standards no figure less qualified to rule, lead, or teach can be imagined, and this consideration surely governs Milton's choice of hero, which requires complete repudiation of the classical virtues as the mark of significant character and potentiality. If we learn by mistakes rather than by ratiocination, as Popper argues, then Samson must necessarily be uniquely qualified for mastery, even though the Chorus with its conventional values sees only the present "abject fortune" to which he is reduced. Yet paradoxically it is precisely their shallow rational- izations that trigger Samson's more powerful intuition. He has already recognized that from the start his career has reflected the grotesquely irrational forces that gov- ern the world:

> God, when he gave me strength, to show withal
> How slight the gift was, hung it in my Hair.
>
> (58-59)

And when the Chorus complacently assumes that Sam- son is simply being punished for betraying Israel by his sexual interest in various "bad Women" from the enemy's camp, he firmly rejects their specious verdict just as he had rejected his parents' advice against his first Philistine marriage:

                                                    they knew not
        That what I motion'd was of God; I knew
        From intimate impulse, and therefore urg'd
        The Marriage on; that by occasion hence
        I might begin Israel's Deliverance,
        The work to which I was divinely call'd.
        She proving false, the next I took to Wife . . .
        I thought it lawful from my former act.

                                              (221-27, 231)

This is a crucial passage for its illustration of the Miltonic view of the categorical imperative, and we may be sure that the use of marriage as the occasion for the discussion of moral imperatives is no accident, as it also strikingly serves the same purpose for Robert Greville, Lord Brooke, in his famous *Discourse*[3] about the English episcopacy—a text which influenced Milton greatly. However, Milton's sense of the issues is even subtler than Brooke's. The initial motivation to marry an enemy is not at first even rationally founded or defended—it depends essentially on "intimate impulse" which is, at best, rationalized after the event. The wry development lies in the fact that while even in defeat Samson still believes his original irrational marriage was divinely sanctioned, he admits that his logical application of his own rationalization to a second such marriage was not so sanctioned. Thus of two exactly similar acts, the first is sanctioned by God, the second, for reasons inaccessible to human logic, is not: a clear indication of the irrelevance of Platonic procedures of analysis, which assume the consistency of universals.

[3] *Discourse*, pp. 22-30. See p. 101.

The Chorus now begins painfully to understand the incommensurable nature of omniscience (or, if we will, of the totality of the cosmos) which must exceed the grasp of mere localized human analysis:

> Just are the ways of God,
> And justifiable to Men;
> Unless there be who think not God at all: . . .
> Yet more there be who doubt his ways not just,
> As to his own edicts, found contradicting,
> Then give the reins to wand'ring thought, . . .
> But never find self-satisfying solution.
> As if they would confine th' interminable,
> And tie him to his own prescript,
> Who made our Laws to bind us, not himself
> And hath full right to exempt
> Whom it pleases him by choice
> From National obstriction, without taint
> Of sin, or legal debt;
> For with his own Laws he can best dispense.
>
> (293-95, 300-2, 306-14)

While the Chorus recognizes that its moral judgments must often be suspended and even intuits a Pauline sense of grace in seeing that God may remit merited punishment, still it also sees the ominous negative corollary which Milton had learned so painfully, that virtue may not be rewarded:

> God of our Fathers, what is man!
> That thou towards him with hand so various,
> Or might I say contrarious,
> Temper'st thy providence through his short course,
> Not evenly, as thou rul'st

Th' Angelic orders and inferior creatures mute,
Irrational and brute.
Nor do I name of men the common rout, . . .
But such as thou hast solemnly elected,
With gifts and graces eminently adorn'd
To some great work, thy glory,
And people's safety, which in part they effect:
Yet toward these, thus dignifi'd, thou oft,
Amidst thir height of noon,
Changest thy count'nance . . .
Unseemly falls in human eye,
Too grievous for the trespass or omission.

                                    (667-74, 678-84, 690-91)

One must admire the vigor of Milton in stating this truth so alien to the naive Christian's sense of Providence. It is this firm recognition of the range and illogicality of human suffering which requires that the play be considered fully tragic. More than most tragedies, it recognizes a universe frequently unresponsive to conventional human expectations of reward. Yet it shows a Shakespearean irony in that while its hero is rewarded for his service by suffering, humiliation and death, it imperceptibly frees him not only of his right to claim reward for merit, but also of the guilt for his betrayals. Samson is given a second chance to redeem each of his failures, and in fact achieves as complete a transcendence of shallow motivation as the Christ of *Paradise Regained*, but without any sense of superhuman ease. The primary agent is Dalila, who plausibly serves to raise all the choices that Christ's Devil had proposed: a life of private satisfaction (914-27), the merits of patriotic public service (849-62), the desire to rule (800-10). However, the ultimate challenge she offers is subtler still: the temptation to slur over the issues in a facile reconciliation with evil and failure. Dalila suggests that human inadequacy is so universal it should simply be accepted and forgotten. Samson in a double response vindicates his moral discrimination: he is relentless in evaluating their shared failure:

> I gave, thou say'st th'example,
> I led the way; bitter reproach, but true,
> I to myself was false ere thou to me;
> Such pardon therefore as I give my folly,
> Take to thy wicked deed.

> (822-26)

The tone suggests the savagely retributive justice often found in the Old Testament, but Samson's last speech to Dalila has, curiously enough, an explicit mercifulness at the core of its abuse: "At distance I forgive thee, go with that; / Bewail thy falsehood." (954-55) Only Dalila's egotistical relapse into hostility may conceal from us the potential for reconciliation in Samson's last proposal. By masking that potential in painful censure, he is able to force into the open Dalila's basic unwillingness to accept her failures and live with and by them.

Dalila is thus like Christ's Devil in fostering an enriched ethical awareness in the hero. Samson's analysis of Dalila's confused motives in her betrayal of him is a masterly definition of all international relationships:

> Being once a wife, for me thou wast to leave
> Parents and country; nor was I their subject,
> Nor under their protection but my own,
> Thou mine, not theirs: if aught against my life

> Thy country sought of thee, it sought unjustly,
> Against the law of nature, law of nations,
> No more thy country, but an impious crew
> Of men conspiring to uphold thir state
> By worse than hostile deeds, violating the ends
> For which our country is a name so dear;
> Not therefore to be obey'd.

> (885-95)

The principle established here is that private ethical relationships are primary, so that national and international regulations may not properly take precedence over domestic claims. This is now broadly recognized, though it has been little practiced in many past and present political systems. It is a truth which only Samson could assert, and only after his own costly choices and mistakes; and it is a paradox hard to rationalize, despite Milton's heroic efforts to do so in his Divorce Pamphlets where he claims that the actual condition of a marital relationship is the only grounds for regulating it, not state or ecclesiastical sanctions. Like Samson, Milton learns from his mistakes, not from the logic he affects by hindsight.

In dealing with the giant Harapha, Samson continues to show his recovered, even advanced, understanding of the nature of the strength which he had betrayed. He sees that his power was not magical or merely physical but psychological, dependent on his trust in God:

> I know no spells, use no forbidden Arts;
> My trust is in the living God who gave me
> At my Nativity this strength, diffus'd
> No less through all my sinews, joints and bones,

Than thine, while I preserv'd these locks unshorn,
The pledge of my unviolated vow. . . .
All these indignities, for such they are
From thine, these evils I deserve and more,
Acknowledge them from God inflicted on me
Justly, yet despair not of his final pardon
Whose ear is ever open; and his eye
Gracious to re-admit the suppliant;
In confidence whereof I once again
Defy thee to the trial of mortal fight.

(1139-44, 1168-75)

It is impressive to recognize how smoothly Milton introduces a New Testament sense of God's mercy into Samson's awareness without violating our sense of Old Testament physical heroism. For Milton establishes that what gives Samson recovered confidence in his strength is a simple intuition that God is on his side again despite his own confessed inadequacies. Faith becomes strength in a literal sense here.

Nor are Samson's recovered resources simply physical; when the timorous Chorus fears official punishment for him at the prompting of the humiliated Harapha, Samson's rejection of the possibility is cool and decisive:

He must allege some cause, and offer'd fight
Will not dare mention, lest a question rise
Whether he durst accept the offer or not,
And that he durst not plain enough appear'd.

(1253-56)

However, such questions are relatively trivial and localized. The climax of the poem, and of Milton's career as a Christian poet, lies rather in Samson's final confrontation, that with the Officer of the Philistine State. Here we reach the most recurrent moral concern in human affairs (which Dalila had first raised): the nature of the obligation of the autonomous individual to the forms of the society in which he finds himself. The Officer requires Samson to participate in the Philistines' celebration of their God Dagon's feast-day:

> Thy strength they know surpassing human rate,
> And now some public proof thereof require
> To honor this great Feast, and great Assembly.
>
> (1313-15)

Samson firmly refuses to participate in acts he considers to be blasphemous: "Our Law forbids at thir Religious Rites, / My presence" (1320-21). He is not moved by threats of punishment and explains to the Chorus that it is one thing to honor Dagon and quite another to serve the Philistines at the mill:

> Not in thir Idol-Worship, but by labor
> Honest and lawful to deserve my food
> Of those who have me in thir civil power.
>
> (1365-67)

This is close to Hobbesian in its mechanical criteria for obedience, and indeed Samson accepts the fact that he would even serve Dagon "where outward force constrains" (1369). But he shows that this is not yet his condition.

So far Samson has pursued a highly pragmatic pattern of behavior limited only by his ultimate refusal to betray his recovered faith in God's will:

Shall I abuse this Consecrated gift
Of strength, again returning with my hair
After my great transgression, so requite
Favor renew'd, and add a greater sin
By prostituting holy things to Idols?

(1354-58)

This appears entirely proper and rational. Yet in fact the argument is suddenly repudiated by Samson without premeditation or constraint or any objective change in his circumstances whatever. From having calmly decided not to go along with the Officer, he abruptly and irrationally declares to the Chorus that he will do so:

Be of good courage, I begin to feel
Some rousing motions in me which dispose
To something extraordinary my thoughts.
I with this Messenger will go along,
Nothing to do, be sure, that may dishonor
Our Law, or stain my vow of Nazarite.
If there be aught of presage in the mind,
This day will be remarkable in my life
By some great act, or of my days the last.

(1381-89)

Here is the existential moment of truth, the unsolicited condescension of God's will to lowly human awareness, and one should note that it is both totally illogical and undefined at its arrival and even as to its outcome, except that it excludes the violation of previously validated existential imperatives, such as the Law of Moses. In other words, the existential imperative does not so much violate existing standards of value as go beyond them, after their scope of operation has been defined and limited. The human mind in its most heroic state is not revolutionary in overthrowing past truths, but humbly expectant of the providential discovery of new ones. As Hamlet said under identical conditions, having exhausted the application of harsh traditional values and before launching on the last uncertain yet decisive phase of his career, "The readiness is all" (V.ii.211). At this point Hamlet also has intuitions of something monumental impending but accepts his own ignorance, for "no man of aught he leaves knows." Hamlet also assents to the absolute and unfathomable Will of God: "There is a special providence in the fall of a sparrow," overtly echoing the Christ of Matthew's Gospel: "Two sparrows sell for a penny, don't they? Yet not a single sparrow falls to the ground without your Father's knowledge. The very hairs of your head are all numbered" (10.29-30, Phillips).

The correctness of Samson's revised analysis is instantly vindicated: having made his intuitive decision he is cleared of immorality or arbitrariness by the course of events before he has to act, for the returning Officer assures him that unless he comes,

> we shall find such Engines to assail
> And hamper thee, as thou shalt come of force
> Though thou wert firmlier fast'n'd than a rock.
>
> (1396-98)

Even by his previous moral and pragmatic standards Samson can now properly say " I am content to go" (1403); but one should note that his initial determination to obey the Phillistines was *not* governed by the sense that it would be improper to allow the Philistines to "trail me through their streets / Like a wild beast" (1402-3), since the threat had not even been made at that point. So, like Hamlet, the social outcast Samson confidently moves off to destroy the Philistine Establishment and himself, without the least sense of how he will do so, and indeed without even the certain knowledge that this will be his role.

The mark of the mind which changes history is thus not philosophic skill in defining the correct means and ends, as the youthful Milton had thought, following Plato. Instead Samson parallels the advice Jesus gives to his disciples in Matthew (10.18-20) when launching them on their missionary career: "You will be brought into the presence of governors and kings . . . but when they do arrest you, never worry about how you are to speak or what you are to say. You will be told at the time what you are to say. For it will not be really you who are speaking but the Spirit of your Father speaking through you" (Phillips). Despite its theological formulation this advice is perfectly intelligible in modern psychology, in terms of the dynamic mental condition it seeks to create. The extraordinary physical prowess of Samson may conceivably be ascribed to this increment from perfect timing in the application of muscular pressure to the pillars of the state. At a given moment a whole Establishment or even a military campaign may be shattered by well-judged local action by an isolated individual. It is a mind so calm and poised that it is alert to every nuance and possibility that flashes upon it moment by moment, and which is therefore quite capable of changing the balance of historical forces by a single but decisive application of pressure when the right occasion occurs. This is the precarious kind of situation reflected in the old nursery rhyme about the loss of a kingdom because of a loose nail in a knight's horseshoe, or of the story of the single wily native turning back a whole army of Barbarians from the environs of Rome by telling them, in a sense truthfully, that it was so distant he had worn out a pair of iron-soled shoes walking to it. At the right moment in time, the way to start the most enduring institution in world history proved to be to gather a tiny handful of rustic nonentities as disciples, and then get oneself executed like a common criminal by the provincial authorities. The ways of Providence, or Fate, or just mere random history cannot be rationally predicted and they transcend conventional ideas of merit in the choice of agents. Yet, unexpectedly therefore, the humble and trusting person wise enough to realize this may soon be in a position to change history.

However, the crucial event itself is not always immediately apparent or intelligible. Thus even Samson's murderous destruction of the Philistine theater proves under investigation to be not quite so merciless and indiscriminate as it seems at first: Samson's intuition has already forbidden the Hebrews to accompany him. Moreover, the theater is occupied only by the drunkenly frenzied leaders of the Philistines, filled "with mad desire / To call in haste for thir destroyer" (1677-78). Thus God proves himself surprisingly discriminating in his punishment: "The vulgar only scap'd who stood without" (1659). It is the Platonic Guardians of the State only who are doomed by their own hubris to a bizarre destruction which they are incapable of predicting. God protects the humble of both nations, and destroys only the merciless tormentors of the wretched.

In this irrational way, the defeated Milton was also
to triumph over his enemies after his death. For the
Stuart Monarchy which he had labored to overthrow
by reason with seeming futility finally collapsed irrecoverably, without argument or even a blow being struck,
in the Glorious Revolution of 1688. The imperceptible
conditioning of English awareness achieved by men like
Milton finally did enable the English to get what they
wanted with a minimum of extravagance, thus averting
from England itself those decades of warfare which
generation after generation of rational or idealistic reformers have inflicted on their homelands throughout
the rest of Europe, in the Age of Revolutions. The
English had learned, like Milton, not to be too idealistic,
confident, or consciously intelligent. Ever since this has
made them seem muddled, hypocritical, and inept—but
it rarely leaves them for long trapped on the wrong side
of historical forces. Perhaps the English political consciousness which slowly evolved in the course of the
tumults and confusion of the seventeenth century comes
closest to being what a sense of Christian politics might
require. At least it evolves in harmony with Milton's
own political and poetic maturation in the face of his
own costly failures:

> All is best, though we oft doubt,
> What th' unsearchable dispose
> Of highest wisdom brings about,
> And ever best found in the close.
> Oft he seems to hide his face,
> But unexpectedly returns
> And to his faithful Champion hath in place
> Bore witness gloriously; whence *Gaza* mourns

And all that band them to resist
His uncontrollable intent;
His servants he with new acquist
Of true experience from this great event
With peace and consolation hath dismist,
And calm of mind, all passion spent.

(1745-58)

Epilogue

The critical axiom governing this essay has been that "context defines content," whether we speak of literature or even of human culture as a whole. By the most elementary priciples of causality, literary achievement is a function of authorial experience, and specifically of the ideas effectively governing an author's personal behavior. Literature can never be rigidly isolated from such aspects of autobiography, and the lack of the kind of helpful biographical congruences I have examined in Milton's life explains why even superior anonymous works require so much more arduous critical effort to establish their worth—as has been the case with *Beowulf, Sir Gawain and the Green Knight,* and the medieval dramatic cycles. In these autobiographical terms it must be recognized that even the present essay is a product of the distinct overlap of personal experience with that of its subject, which extends far beyond its development in the shades beneath Milton's mulberry tree in Christ's College garden (while savoring the same bittersweet fruit which he might have tasted). As a graduate of Cambridge I find that my three years at Emmanuel College, "the great nursery of puritan thought,"[1] have deeply condi-

[1] Bush, p. 342.

tioned my own awareness of those same Cambridge Platonists whose influence clearly extended to Milton even after he left the adjacent college of Christ's. Emmanuel's chapel has preserved something of the decorous fervor of the earlier seventeenth-century puritans, as if the stained glass portraits of worthies like Benjamin Whichcote or Peter Sterry, by looking down on the crowded congregations, had also subtly tinctured their complexions in the more archaic sense of that term. This inherited empathy for rational enthusiasm was powerfully reinforced by Basil Willey's urbane expositions of the virtues of the more liberal puritans. More generally, their tone and attitudes deeply condition our modern awareness through numerous literary and intellectual influences including not only Milton and Marvell, or Browne and Brooke, but extending at least as far as Locke and Newton, not to mention the liberal wing of American puritanism. Such figures as the seventeenth-century graduate of Emmanuel, John Harvard, founded the great American institutions of higher learning, and the precedents which they afforded evolved into the enlightened zeal which still characterizes, albeit fadingly, the best indigenous American intellectual tradition. However, over the years I have come to fear that this honorable and truly Academic tradition is no longer viable, in part because it is not puritan enough: it overestimates human capacity both objectively and subjectively and the result is paradoxically constricting both to society and the human mind.

Many years ago, in first learning to place Milton in this intellectual tradition under the sane and amiable guidance of Joan Bennett, I found no problem in recognizing and admiring Milton's intellectual congruence with the largely rationalistic philosophy pervading his Renaissance environment, at least in his earlier works. Though I have become very skeptical about the comprehensiveness of its values, I still fully accept Milton's dependence on them in his early career, as formulated by the most recent scholarship. My specific point in the present book has been to stress that this phase of Milton's thinking no longer seems so profoundly distinctive or valuable to us today; nor does it carry over very substantially into his last three major poems, even though there "for many years the tendency of Miltonic criticism has been to stress Milton as a humanist rather than as a Puritan,"[2] so that Martin Larson could sweepingly speak of "Milton's rationalism and repudiation of puritan dogma."[3] The result of this "Platonic" approach to the last poems has been to distort their emphases. It pays almost excessive attention to their traditional rationalism and classic structure instead of to their unique elements of spontaneity, which result from their recognition of unsolicited intuition as a creative principle and of the power of nonrational redemptive forces. Thus the aging Milton has been forced into the same constricting mold as the naively inadequate reformer he once was, with the result that he is still presented as no less rigid, archaic, and aloof to normal human nature than he was in *Comus*. The inadequacy of this restrictive view of Milton as "the last Elizabethan" appears in his actual influence on English tradition, which leads out

[2] Grace, p. 50.

[3] Martin A. Larson, *The Modernity of Milton* (Chicago: University of Chicago Press, 1927), p. 89.

of Neoclassicism and into Blake and the Romantics, authors who scarcely advocate a naive trust in conventional human rationalism and order. Milton has a unique role in this evolution to which scholarship has not yet done full justice.

There is perhaps an alternative scholarly emphasis to the traditional one, available in Stanley Fish's view of an aged and disillusioned Milton setting his admonitory traps for the unwary reader in order to provoke salutary repetitions of Milton's own self-deception; but Milton's ultimate achievement does not seem to me adequately summed up as the repudiation of the rigors of Platonism in order to replace them with an equally rigid and more sadistic Calvinism.[4] Milton's final worldview is his own, and not any mere orthodoxy, such as C. A. Patrides sees in the final works.[5] In them it is Milton's unique blend of a tolerant but wholly disillusioned acceptance of human fallibility with a startling trust in an ultimately benevolent providence which seems likely to prove most valuable to the disoriented modern mind. As Paul Hazard has shown in *The Crisis of the European Conscience*, the admirable if complacent faith in their own reasonableness which even the Independent Puritans and Levellers shared with their Anglican opponents became the norm of modern thought among intellectuals, with the results that this necessarily invites: the cycle of idealism leading to revolution, and then to repression and despairing disillu-

[4] Stanley Fish, *Surprised by Sin: the Reader in "Paradise Lost"* (New York: St. Martin's Press, 1967).

[5] C. A. Patrides, *Milton and the Christian Tradition* (Oxford: Clarendon Press, 1966).

sion which we see anticipated by the earlier career of Milton. The cycle is intrinsic to our Age of Revolution, but it is now simply too archaic and destructive to be allowed to survive unchallenged among educated men. A correct appreciation of Milton's major verse is one excellent way to invite awareness of the more invigorating and creative alternatives. These alternatives are analogous to the order visualized very recently by Karl Popper himself in once again rejecting a rationally constricted universe: "we live in an open universe. We could not make this discovery before there was human knowledge. But once we have made the discovery there is no reason to think that the openness depends exclusively upon the existence of human knowledge. It is much more reasonable to reject all views of a closed universe— that of a causally as well as a probabilistically closed universe. . . . Our universe is partly causal, partly probabilistic, and partly open: it is emergent."[6] It is toward this invigorating sense of a cosmos which eludes the repressive restraints both of Platonic rationalism and Calvinistic determinism that Milton's greatest poetry is directed. For the mature Milton, human nature is never fully master of itself or its environment, for to be so would be to deny the satisfying possibility of a continually enriched awareness which is the best guarantee of a providential principal in creation. The costs of such an open system are great, but never as great as those of the restrictive, solipsistic alternatives, which are themselves often the principal sources of the constraints, violence, and destruction so frequently used

[6] Karl R. Popper, "Indeterminism is Not Enough," *Encounter*, XL, 4 (April, 1973), 20-26.

to argue against the value of the world as we know it. His intuition of this inspiring yet skeptical vision of the human role has kept Milton in the forefront of literary figures to this day, despite the inhibiting terms which some critics have derived from his prose and applied too narrowly to his verse. It is to reiterate this true and positive value of Milton's poetry that this book has been written.

I cannot possibly do justice to the broad range of debts reflected in these pages, from the supervisions with Joan Bennett and the lectures of David Daiches at Cambridge, and my tutorials with J. B. Leishman at Oxford in the fifties to more recent discussions with colleagues like Stephen Orgel and above all Wayne Shumaker here at Berkeley. I should not forget my many students of the sixties who often shared both Milton's youthful idealism and its inevitable disillusionment. Not least I must express my appreciation to my wife for her sustained interest and help in innumerable ways. Of course, many institutions have supported my studies to a crucial extent, above all financially and bibliographically: the University of California's Humanities Institute, the Cambridge University Library, the Bodleian Library, the British Museum, the Huntington Library, the Clark Library, and the British Institute in Florence. All those with whom I have worked in such contexts have shown a consistent patience and goodwill in assisting a project which may often have seemed to them as intemperately iconoclastic and absolutist as the idealistic, earlier Milton at his worst. I can only hope my readers will approach the final text with the same wry sense of the limitations of human nature, and the same serene determination to make the best of things, however painful and seemingly fallen beyond remedy, which it seems to me were part of Milton's own final and exemplary state of mind.

Berkeley, May 1973

Index